THE
MATURE SPIRIT

THE
MATURE
SPIRIT

RELIGION WITHOUT SUPERNATURAL HOPES

By Philip Mayer

Introduction by Vincent Harding
Foreword by Homer A. Jack

PITTENBRUACH PRESS
NORTHAMPTON, MA 01060

Library of Congress Catalog No. 87-61364
ISBN 0-938875-08-6

First Printing 1987   Printed in USA
10 9 8 7 6 5 4 3 2

Published by
PITTENBRUACH PRESS, 15 Walnut St., PO Box 553
                    Northampton, MA 01061

To

my sister,

Doris

(1898–1975)

and

my wife,

Eleanor

TABLE OF CONTENTS

Philip Mayer

BIOGRAPHICAL FOREWORD

    The history of the individual often sums up the history of the race. "The Mature Spirit" demonstrates the evolution of the religious thought of the author. Philip Mayer started as a relative conservative, theologically, and ends up a relative radical. However, the author has not revealed the full circumstances -- the institutional habitat -- of his religious evolution.

    Philip Mayer grew up as a Methodist in Ohio. His grandfather and father were Methodist ministers as were his two brothers. He began his vocational career in Singapore, where for four years he was a Methodist missionary. For the past thirty-one years he has lived in Swarthmore, Pennsylvania, where he is a member of the Society of Friends, a Quaker.

i

In between, Mayer served as pastor not only of Methodist, but also of Congregationalist, Disciples, Universalist, and Humanist churches. For many years, and to this day, he has held fellowship as an accredited Unitarian Universalist clergyman.

He has been a peace activist, associated with the Fellowship of Reconciliation and with such peace personalities as George Paine and Richard Gregg in Boston, A. J. Muste, and Ammon Hennacy of the Catholic Worker movement.

Others who have made a difference in his intellectual life include John Dewey, Edwin Wilson, Vida Scudder, Brand Blanshard, and Henry Cadbury.

He taught at William Penn College in Iowa, and in a Doukhobor community in Canada. He published, if not for the millions, at least for the cognoscenti, "The Walden Round Robin" and "A Primitive Gospel."

In addition to being a pastor, activist, author, editor and teacher, Philip Mayer has at various times made an honest living as a WPA adult education supervisor, a farmer, and a photographer.

These rich, diverse experiences and associations are subtly reflected in this volume.

"The Mature Spirit" recounts the evolution of a universal Quaker. Yet the author ends up not too distant from some modern Methodists. Philip Mayer has come a long way, but middle-of-the-road Protestantism has traveled a long way also in this century. It has not yet caught up with Mayer, but we live in that kind of world. Nothing stands still.

"The Mature spirit" is not the orthodox spirit. The human spirit, for the author, may be the fruit of religious naturalism, but on Mayer's tree the fruit is attractive, not hard and dry. It is the living spirit.

The religion of the future is at hand, immediately available for praxis.

-- Homer A. Jack
Unitarian clergyman
and peace activist

Swarthmore, PA
August 21, 1987

INTRODUCTION

I first met Phil Mayer nearly a decade ago at Pendle Hill, the Quaker-sponsored retreat and study center located a mile or so down the hill and through the woods from Phil's and Eleanor's Swarthmore home. Indeed, soon after we joined the Pendle Hill residential staff, Rosemarie Harding and I heard about the septuagenarian who managed at least once a week, and often more, to walk and climb down the wooded hillside from the Swarthmore College campus to attend the weekday Meeting for Worship at Pendle Hill -- and then, sometimes refusing offers of automobile rides, climbed back up again.

More than once I accompanied Phil on the walking, climbing journey back up to Swarthmore, and I was deeply impressed by the sheer tenacious determination of this man in his late seventies as he clambered up the steep hill, accepting as little help as possible, catching his breath while carrying on stimulating conversation. Clearly it is that marvelous, indomitable spirit which is one of Phil Mayer's great gifts to us, and it is necessary to recognize this book as both substance of and testimony to the compassionate "great-heartedness" which Phil celebrates and manifests in his life -- both on and off the hillside.

In other words, I am convinced that Philip Mayer is a prime example of "The Mature Spirit" of these pages. For decades now, in words and deeds, he has pressed in every possible way the essential double question of the book: What are the elements of the human spirit which are absolutely necessary for the survival of the human community and for the flowering of democratic institutions -- and how do we nurture such life-fulfilling aspects of our being?

Central to the reflections in the book is Philip's crucial conviction: "For the survival of humanity we must learn to cultivate the spirit as freely as we educate the mind." Much of the work is therefore an encouragement "to strive" for the development among us of compassion, love, responsibility and discipline, all moving us toward the flowering of spiritual maturity.

As Philip sees it (rightly, I believe), true religion is meant to aid in every possible way our search for that deep maturity. As a result, much of the work is shaped by his corollary conviction that "Civilization flounders because religion has encouraged false hopes, rather than maturity."

By "religion" Phil Mayer most often tends to mean main-stream European and Euro-American Christianity; as a result, he neglects much "religion" of the majority peoples of the world, including important contributions to a fusing of "naturalism" and "supernaturalism" which have been made by the aboriginals of this hemisphere, the peoples of Africa and those in many parts of India and Asia. (For instance, is "enlightenment" the same as "maturity"? Are those who celebrate the "Great Spirit" in the lakes and the trees and revere "The Great Mystery" beyond lakes and trees to be called "naturalistic" or "supernaturalistic" -- or do they defy these categories?)

Of course it is crucial for us to realize that Phil is picking up many of the debates which raged in religious circles during his own most active years in ministry and service. It would have been good if we could have also had some reflections from Phil on the post-World War II influence of eastern religions among us, or on the religious significance of the "human potential" movement of the last quarter century.

However, whatever the missing pieces, and whatever the debates I might carry on privately with my dear elder brother, there is no doubt that he is one of those marvelous "pioneers of light" who tried to live out his convictions ahead of the time when they spread among the rest of us. For if this wisdom has begun to be shared more widely in our time, then we must surely thank the Phil Mayers among us for the many hills they climbed before we began to join them. Now we may gratefully climb (and dance) together with Phil -- and with sisters and brothers of every religious community -- in our own continuing personal and social quest for what he calls "the fulfillment of the spiritual potentials of humanity."

Vincent Harding
Professor of Religion and Social Transformation
Iliff School of Theology
Denver, Colorado

September 9, 1987

PREFACE

Traditionally, religion has been based on the hope of securing the guidance and support of a supernatural God, that is, a God so all-powerful that he could set aside the orderly ways of nature and rule arbitrarily. This supernaturalistic idea was so firmly fixed that some of the New Testament writers thought God was to be known only in violations of the natural order.

Apparently Jesus did not agree, for many of his parables report observations of nature and declare them to be the ways of God. Part II of this book is devoted entirely to a naturalistic study of Jesus.

Nevertheless, traditional, or "orthodox," religion is still based on the hope of supernatural care and guidance. It is often supposed that there can be no real religion without firm belief in a supernatural God.

The Twentieth century began with a religious movement called "modernism." It was an effort to escape wishful self-deception by doing away with miracles and arbitrary authority in religion.

However, it supposed that it could retain a "personal" God as being as natural as a personal human being, or a life in heaven as being as natural as a life on earth.

A naturalistic first cause has to be a totally undeveloped potential; the intelligence for wise choices and decisions requires experience and growth. It would be "super-natural" for wisdom to appear without experience.

Now, after fifty years of trying to make the new supernaturalism acceptable, there are signs that this "neo-orthodoxy" is breaking up. The secular religion of Harvey Cox, the liberation theology of the basic hispanic communities, the "new reformation" of Bishop James Robinson, the process theology of Whitehead, the "post-theistic thinking" of Thomas Dean, "religious humanism" and many other innovations testify to the present dissatisfaction with traditional Christianity.

The hope of obtaining the favor of an all-powerful God still dominates religious thought, yet the existence of such a God is no longer taken for granted.

The implications of rejecting such a hope have alarmed many people, yet the characteristics of a naturalistic religion are now taking shape. Are they more frightening than the implications of supernaturalism? At least we can now compare the two views and decide for ourselves.

The orthodox view of religion has commonly been marked by the second class status it gives to practical concerns. Issues of peace, race, poverty, and family-planning have been permitted in the church parlors, but many of the devout have felt that the sanctuary of the church should not be profaned by the affairs of this world: "people seek religion to make peace with God, not with men."

There is much to be said for that point of view if "God" is an all-powerful person who needs no help from us in setting the world right. But if "god" is a natural creative cause, limited by conditions which we help to create, then we are needed. Religious cultivation of the human spirit is important.

The religion of the future will not be absorbed in holding people to past beliefs about the spirit, but in cultivating the spirit itself within all people so that it will be more functional.

This is the naturalistic reformation which is now taking place. The purpose of this book is to help in understanding the implications and significance of this re-formation.

My first chapter attempts to orient the reader into religion-without-magic by offering a brief review of the history of religious naturalism. We are indebted to a long line of prophets and teachers from Jesus through Emerson to Einstein and Dewey, who without entering fully into the promised land of "religion without supernaturalism," opened a pathway toward it.

In this preface I would like to mention some of the philosophers and ministers who helped me publish "The Walden Round Robin" from 1942-1948, the forerunner of this book.

The "Robin" was a monthly newsletter exploring the naturalistic religious ideas then being developed. John Dewey offered to serve on the editorial board, along with Brand Blanshard of Yale, Edwin Burtt of Cornell, Arthur Morgan of Antioch, Max Otto of Wisconsin, Henry Wieman of Chicago, and a number of ministers, including Bernard Clausen, Lester Mondale, Kenneth Patton, and Edwin Wilson.

I also want to thank neighbors and friends who have helped with the manuscript. In particular I thank Professors Monroe Beardsley, Thomas

Dean, and Willard Richan of Temple University, Rudolph Hirsch and John Honnold of the University of Pennsylvania, Stephen Croddy of West Chester State University, Patrick Henry and John Moore of Swarthmore College, and the now-deceased theologians Henry Cadbury of Harvard, and Alexander Purdy of Hartford Seminary, whose homes were in this area.

The continuing interest of Thomas McCormick, Michael Ritzman, and John Seybold has sustained me. Wilma Mosholder, a retired theological school librarian, has gone over many versions of the manuscript. Most of all, my wife, Eleanor, has been constant in giving whatever help I needed.

The task of developing and sorting out the various strands of naturalistic religion has been life-long and exciting; the writing has been slow and laborious. I have persisted in the hope that this effort might help us all find the magnanimity of spirit which fulfills life.

P.F.M.

215 College Avenue
Swarthmore, PA 19081
August, 1987

THE MATURE SPIRIT

PART I

THE NATURALISTIC BASIS FOR RELIGION

PART I

A NATURALISTIC BASIS FOR RELIGION

Chapter 1: THE HUMAN SPIRIT

One morning during the Winter Olympics at Sarajevo, ski champion Phil Mahre was being interviewed on television as to his strenuous preparations for the day's events. Finally the reporter asked, "What are you wishing for the day?"

Instead of wishing for the prize, Phil's mind turned to the news, just received, that back in America his wife was in labor giving birth to their second child. His face contorted in pain. Fighting back the tears he answered, "I wish I were home."

The incident gave a glimpse, not only into the emotions of the athlete, but also into the spirit that makes us all human, and in the best sense religious.

Each of us has the potential for such a spirit; we could have a nation of responsible people, with homes that are loving, and cities that are models of good citizenship. Instead we spend trillions of dollars on armaments and find ourselves unable to halt cultural decay. Lack of great-heartedness threatens our very existence.

The survival of feelings such as Phil had is endangered in modern society by the pressure to sacrifice everything for material success, physical security, or religious tradition.

As a result we are producing creatures who look human, but who do not have the compassion, or the appreciation for others, which characterize human beings. No one wants to live like a dog, or other brute animal, with no feeling for music, sunsets or friendly communication, yet that is the kind of creature we are in danger of becoming.

Our religious institutions should help us cultivate the human spirit, but our clergy appears to have thought that it was more important to strengthen the power and authority of the church.

When people supposed that their religions were founded by a supernatural God, they assumed that their dogmas were guaranteed to be accurate and that if they preserved the dogmas, God would make everything else come out right. This belief strengthened authoritarianism but weakened respect for differing opinions.

Like the German Nazis, we are more aware of physical dangers than we are of the threat to our humanity. The Nazis were eliminated because the human race was not willing to return to a brute existence. The German churches of the 1930's were strong enough to prevent the destruction of their spirit and nation, but they didn't. They were more interested in maintaining faith in their creeds than they were in preserving the human spirit.

Traditionally, religions have rejected concern for the human spirit as "secular," for it turned people from thoughts of heaven, to an interest in this world. When people believed in a supernatural God, they thought earthly matters could be left to him; faithful believers would enjoy eternal bliss regardless of what happened in this world.

"Spirit" as I am using the term is not an invisible person, such as a ghost, a soul, or a gremlin. Instead, "spirit" is the invisible feeling of persons but it is not detachable from a person, or able to float around in space at will. The spirit has physical force only as it acts through the person who has that spirit.

The "human spirit" is an understanding or sympathetic feeling toward other people and things. It includes love, but it is not supernatural. Contrary to the opinion of the Apostle

Paul, I see love often failing. It is like seed which may be sown on stony ground and produce nothing. We plant love because it is human to do so, and if we don't plant, we get only weeds.

In rejecting the hope of a supernatural guarantee that love, or other expressions of the spirit, will succeed, I am aligning myself with those whose outlook is called "naturalistic."

Most religions of the past were supernaturalistic, claiming the guarantee of a power beyond nature. The survival of humanity depends on our spiritual growth. We must be secularists planting love on earth in order to survive. This requires only the utilization of forces within the natural order.

The human spirit does not claim infallibility or perfection. Although to err is human, we are not content to blame failure on human nature, for it is human nature to seek the causes of failure and to correct them.

Naturalism promises very little as compared with supernaturalism, which promises everything. Nevertheless we are learning some positive results of a natural spirituality. For example, we find that the human spirit is expressed, not only in compassion for the poor, but also in an attitude of respect for people of other nations, races, and creeds.

This attitude of respect for differences is

the aspect of the human which we call "the democratic spirit." Ancient people knew democracy as
government by the people, but they had not yet
grasped the essential spirit of democracy.

This new spirit is most evident in the United
States Congress, where respect for opponents is
strictly enforced. It is beginning to be recognized as a necessary ingredient of any democracy,
and of any religious spirit. It is important
because it enables us to move forward together in
a way that was impossible when everyone claimed
supernatural authority and infallibility. The
democratic spirit is needed for evolution and
growth, even in religion.

Perhaps this summary of what "the human spirit" means will be clarified by my devoting the
remainder of this introductory chapter to a brief
review of the way naturalistic religion has developed historically.

The Beginning of Religious Naturalism

In the naturalistic view, religion is not a
matter of developing a relationship with a
supernatural or magical God, but of maturing the
spiritual potential, or "god," that is in everyone. Therefore a history of religion begins, not
with an account of the origins of superstition,
but with the evolution of spiritual qualities.

The spirit which distinguishes people from brute animals was not handed to mankind fully formed and perfect. Its development took time and effort, similar to the slow and laborious growth of a child. To expect that an appeal to Buddha, Allah, Jehovah, or any other God will give us spiritual maturity by command, is to expect primitive magic.

Evolution had developed a degree of love, loyalty, responsibility, and other spiritual qualities in brutes before humanoids appeared. Religion is a conscious commitment to a continuation of that maturing process.

Early in the history of mankind, a few individuals realized that their needs could not be met by incantation or ritual. For example, some American Indians were aware of "a great spirit" in nature, and they tried to live in harmony with it. Their freedom from superstition gave them exceptional dignity and maturity.

In contrast, supernaturalistic ideas probably began with a sense of helplessness. People did not understand lightning and as a result they stood in fear before a God of thunder, and worshipped it.

Fear and mystery do not increase one's love, responsibility, understanding, or other spiritual powers. Instead, they are the attitudes out of which belief in superstitions emerge.

The main religions of the Orient were originally naturalistic. Both Confucianism and Buddhism swept aside the worship of supernaturalistic Gods, while for Hinduism and Taoism god was a natural force.

Unfortunately, Orientals often supposed that to live naturally was to live like the lilies of the field, without striving; still, the rise of Oriental civilization was paralleled by the emergence of a form of naturalism, and the decline of the Orient was partly the cause and partly the result of a revived supernaturalism.

The ancient Greeks and Romans were polytheists, but belief in many gods of seas and mountains may be less handicapping than belief in a single supernatural God.

Jesus drew most of his lessons from observations of nature. He insisted that human goals could be achieved by loving the enemy, not by hoping for supernatural liberation. Yet the Gospels, which were written by the Messianists who expected magical deliverance, pictured Jesus as the false prophet he had condemned.

This produced dark ages during which learning decayed, doubters were massacred, and theologians quarreled over trivialities.

The Renaissance and Reformation were intellectual awakenings which weakened the destructive power of supernaturalism. This led, in the eighteenth century, to the development of a naturalistic doctrine called "deism."

It held that although the creation of the world needed a supernatural God, ordinary living required acceptance of natural requirements. This was similar to the view attributed to Jesus, that although God has supernatural power it is wrong to expect him to use it (Luke 4.12).

Deism had a seriously limited concept of nature, but nevertheless it was widely accepted. The American colonial churches and their clergy revolted from the tyranny of supernaturalism before they revolted from the king. Washington, Franklin, Jefferson, Adams, Paine, and many others were deists.

The Declaration of Independence based its claims on "the laws of Nature and of Nature's God." Our democracy would have been impossible without this liberating influence.

At the beginning of the nineteenth century, romantic writers such as Wordsworth and Emerson thought of god as the inspirational aspect of nature. This poetic view was largely dispelled in 1857 when Charles Darwin discovered the principles of evolution. Darwin's picture of the creative process led many to think of nature as cruel.

Religious thought in the 20th century

Modernism. The twentieth century began with a religious movement called "modernism." Darwin's observations were so well supported that the more alert preachers found his principles inescapable. A way had to be found to reconcile theology with this new understanding.

Discontent with the old dogmas became so great that when Protestant leaders began to accept evolution, it created a remarkable religious revival. Capable men were attracted to the ministry. The social gospel was preached. Young Men's and Young Women's Christian Associations were built. Religious settlements were established in the slums. Religion flourished on the campuses, and missionaries were sent by the hundreds to foreign countries.

From Fosdick the Baptist, McConnell the Methodist, Rufus Jones the Quaker, to Teilhard de Chardin the Catholic, modernism was adopted by informed church people.

Although the modernists were striving toward naturalism, they thought that a conscious God was as natural as a conscious man, that a conscious heaven was as natural as a conscious life on earth. But when the supernaturalistic implications of these assumptions became apparent, modernism expired.

Looking back on the gifted preachers of that period, it is difficult to see why they still adhered to supernaturalistic concepts of god, salvation, and death.

From my own more humble experiences at the time, I think the trouble was that we were not prepared to meet human need without the popular supernatural hopes. We knew that nature in its conscious forms is uncaring, and we were not prepared to accept our responsibility for developing the spirit of care.

We knew that the source of our humanity was the potential for love, but we still supposed that it had been fully developed in the beginning; we did not see that the value of life comes only as we bring this potential into fulfillment.

Besides our own limitations, four other factors contributed to the collapse of modernism: (a) the rise of a ruthless fundamentalist inquisition which purged many modernists from positions of influence; (b) the great depression made compromises necessary to meet expenses; (c) the rise of Nazism, and two world wars, necessitated the postponement of theological problems; (d) the development of a more accurate naturalism made the compromises of modernism inadequate. It was suddenly realized that if a supernatural God could appear without evolution, there would have been no need for evolution.

Neo-orthodoxy. When modernism faltered, Karl Barth was ready to revive supernaturalism in a retrenched form which came to be known as "neo-orthodoxy." It was not a complete retreat to fundamentalism, for it accepted evolution and rejected the physical miracles. Although it recognized that many of the biblical stories are myths, yet it insisted that a supernatural God could be revealed and explained only in myths.

Any myth which makes truth clearer is useful; the Christian myth would be acceptable if it were true that our source is a separate, supernatural God whom we must worship to protect our destiny. But if our source is the potential for love and democratic maturity, then the traditional myths are misleading.

Instead of providing incentives for the kind of spiritual development we need, neo-orthodoxy offered the idea that spirituality is a matter of communicating with a supernatural spirit. This supplied a sedative for distress but offered no challenge to personal responsibility; it strengthened the church but weakened the people.

Fortunately, the main-line churches are awakening to the resulting losses they have sustained. The fifty-year period of neo-orthodox compromise may be drawing to a close.

John Dewey (1859-1952) realized that all things, good or bad, the spiritual as well as the physical, are natural. His only religious book, "A Common Faith" (Yale 1934) made no effort to outline a theological position, but he urged some religious people to make explicit the implications of the universalism of nature. That is my purpose, especially in chapters two, three, and four.

M. K. Gandhi (1869-1948). For me, Mahatma Gandhi has been the most helpful religious naturalist. Granted that he followed many superstitious Hindu customs, such as cow reverence, yet he was not inhibited by Judeo-Christian supernaturalism. The common Hindi word for god is "sat," which means "truth," "reality," "source," or "spiritual potential." Gandhi had no supernatural expectations; he depended on "sat-yagraha," "truth-force" or "soul-force." Truth did not have a separate being; it needed people to give it expression. He said:

> Truth is perhaps the most important name of God. In fact it is more correct to say that Truth is God, than to say that God is Truth... All our activities should be centered in Truth... Truth should be the very breath of our life. When...once we learn how to apply this never-failing test of Truth (reality), we will be able to find out what is worth doing, what is worth seeing, and what is

worth reading... There is no place in
it for cowardice, no place for de-
feat. -- M. K. Gandhi, "From Yerav-
da Mandir," Desai, Ahmedabad, 1932,
pp. 1-4.

Gandhi saw god, soul-force, or truth as a
potential within ourselves which we can and should
fulfill. It was not a separate power to be coaxed
into doing things for us. (For further discussion
of Gandhi, see below, pp 134.)

The Current Religious Situation

At present, religious thought is confused.
Society is in a state of cultural shock. It has
not learned how to cope with the nuclear threat,
and it is bewildered by the new science. Many
people are losing their grip on reality. They are
turning to astrology, fundamentalism, even witch-
craft. Seldom has the public been more suscept-
ible to unrealistic beliefs. Even the professional theologians have been paralyzed. The travail
of bringing new religious conceptions to birth has
been dangerous.

Fortunately, the main-line churches are beginning to realize that their reversion to supernaturalism is in large measure responsible for the
turmoil. Liberals in the Quaker, Unitarian,
Jesuit, and other religious societies are begin-

ning to grope for more universalistic formulations of the spiritual outlook. People are discovering that evolution has provided them with the potential for spiritual maturity.

This is more important than the discovery of nuclear power, for only the growth which results from spiritual understanding can free mankind from the limitations of a primitive and barbaric past.

Of course the evolved spiritual potential within us does not tell us exactly what to do; it does not save us by grace, or answer our prayers, but it does provide us with the capacity to love, to understand, to appreciate, to be responsible, democratic, and magnanimous. The churches are beginning to abandon their supernaturalistic claims, and to focus instead on cultivating the guidance of the spirit which gives religion and life their significance.

In view of the present peril to human survival which the possibility of nuclear war has raised, Gordon Kaufman, Professor of Divinity at Harvard, says it is obvious that man can no longer hope for supernatural salvation; human responsibility must now be accepted in full. This forces upon us radical changes in our religious thinking:

> The personalistic conception of God,
> so powerfully presented by the tradi-
> tional images of Christian and Jewish
> piety, seems less and less defensible

in the face of the issues humanity today confronts. -- Gordon D. Kaufman; reprinted by permission from the Harvard Divinity Bulletin, Vol. 13/#3 (1983), p. 8.

Since we can no longer hope for supernatural protection, it has become imperative that religion give up its absorption in the mysteries which its theory of a supernatural God has created. It must begin to take seriously the task of seeing to it that everyone has the opportunity to fulfill his or her life -- to fulfill the spiritual potential which creates our humanity.

With this brief introduction, let us, in the next three chapters, seek the naturalistic answers to the three main religious questions: (1) what is our source; (2) what are the requirements for life; and (3) what is our goal or end?

Chapter 2: THE SOURCE OF LIFE

Identifying the Source

The Bible begins with a story of creation, partly to answer questions about the source of all things, but also on the logical assumption that, to achieve the good, one must live in harmony with whatever is responsible for producing it.

In ancient times, people often supposed that the world had been made the way a person makes things; a man first has an idea of the house he wants to build and then he hammers his materials together according to his plan. There was little knowledge of the principles of evolution on which a different concept of the creative process could be based.

With greater understanding of evolution, the world no longer appears to be the work of a separate, external being, but the product of inner, developing potentials, somewhat like the potentials within a seed, or an infant.

Evolutionary theory further suggests (a) that in the beginning this inner source was totally undeveloped, since any development would indicate that there had been an earlier evolutionary beginning; we must start our explanations, not with a mature mind and spirit, but with the totally undeveloped potentials for these qualities, (b) that evolution would have been more rapid and less cruel if there had been conscious guidance or if the design could have been prepared in advance, and (c) that the goals of life are to be won by fulfilling significant inner potentials, rather than by winning the favor of an external creator.

This new understanding does not decrease the importance of the source, but instead of finding it enthroned in heaven, we see it as the inner potential in all things.

Modern science implies a source so different from ancient concepts that many people suppose that it eliminates God entirely. Indeed, if the word "God" means a supernatural person who could order the world into existence, then the new view does eliminate God. However, some people define "god" as any concept of the causal source.

Our religions generally have supposed that the source and power for good is a separate and supernatural being. In contrast, naturalists believe that original energy is like all power in having potentials for either good or evil, depending on how the power is used.

I would like to employ the word "god" with a small impersonal "g" to mean, not a separate person who willfully determines the good, but the natural potential for good to be found in all energy, particularly the potential for the goal or good of human life -- spiritual maturity. It should be the function of religion to subordinate potentials for evil and to cultivate potentials for good.

The older view of God as a man-like person was supported by the primitive belief in unseen spirits, such as devils of disease, or a god of lightning. Love had no power except as a separate spirit of love gave it power. Of course love has no power except as a person feels and practices love, but that does not make it a separate person. St. Theresa suggested that god, the potential for love, has no hands, feet, or lips but ours.

The perennial recurrence of belief in unseen spirits and of myths about them has been offered as proof of their reality, or, at least, of their psychological necessity. To be sure, fairy tales are always popular; recurring myths do uncover perennial hopes, but they may be the crippling hopes which are mistaken and that discourage serious effort. Myths demonstrate the need for explanations, but they do not prove that the mythological explanations are valid or helpful.

God. Although many people have given up the idea of a manlike God, yet there is still confusion between the older view of the source as a separate being, and the evolutionary view of the source as an inner potential. Paul Tillich pointed out that the idea of the source as a separate person produces belief in an authoritarian God, an inerrant scripture, a supernatural salvation, and a religion devoted to rituals for praising an almighty benefactor:

> The demonic god... who appears throughout the history of religion is a being beside others... a being with an absolute claim... a demon with a divine name. He indeed is the principle of all heteronomous [external]... authorities from the family tyrant to the tyrant who conquers the world... God is not a being, but the ground of all being. -- Paul Tillich, "Authority and Revelation," reprinted by permission from Harvard University Bulletin, Vol. 49/#8 (1952), p. 36.

Or, we might say, god is not a person but the potential for all mature personality. Henri

Bergson took literally the analogy between an evolutionary potential and a seed. Both represent potentials, but the seed has already evolved the pattern of its goal, whereas evolution is like an electrical potential, ready to be put to any use for which channels are open. If evolution were like a seed it would need a supernatural God to do the predetermining.

Spirit. Supernaturalists use the word Spirit (capital S) to mean an unseen being, a God; Spirituality is reverence for such a Spirit. In contrast I shall use "spirit" with a small 's' to mean attitudes or feelings such as love, responsibility, appreciation or democracy.

As in my use of the word 'god,' the capital letter is used for the supernaturalistic meaning which I reject. Many writers capitalize their own God but use lower case for pagan gods, but in my view the capitalization should stand for a personification.

Supernaturalists may believe that nature offers only blind chance and brute impulses as guides and authorities. They forget that nature has given us, in evolutionary history, a great wealth of experience in spiritual development. Biblical or priestly authority diverts attention away from the more perfect guidance of spiritual experience.

Potentials and their Development

In an engineering sense, a potential is a measurable amount of pressure ready to be applied to anything. In contrast, a human potential is an immeasurable capacity to do certain specific things, such as thinking, loving, or playing the piano.

However, this is only a difference in form; all energy is of one interchangeable kind or nature. The food which supplies energy for our brains could have been burned in a locomotive to pull a train.

Yet there is a difference. The energy of inorganic activities does not feel the need for survival or renewal, whereas the energy of organisms is spent in large part on survival, renewal, and maturing. The drive to fulfill the human pattern of magnanimous maturity is felt as a spiritual hunger which prompts human action.

People sometimes ask, "Who made the potential?" This is like asking, "Who made god?"

Since nothing could create existence which did not already exist, it follows that the power to manifest existence is an uncaused necessity of the fact that something exists. It is an axiom of physics that energy can neither be created nor destroyed; it can only be changed from one form to another, such as from heat to electricity.

As yet, we cannot trace all details in the process by which the undeveloped potentials of space-time are transformed into material particles, and on into the human drive for fulfilling the patterns of human maturity.

It has been suggested that some beginning steps in the process may have been observed in the behavior of cosmic rays. These rays emerge at maximum velocity from all parts and periods of space-time, and in quantities large enough to replace all the energy dissipated by the stars.

We are just beginning to understand how these particles of energy are melded together under the velocities and temperatures of original motion. Perhaps eventually we shall understand the constant renewal of the universe through such manifestations of the pressures of existence.

The further development of these potentials is better understood in biological evolution. Each member of a species drives to fulfill the pattern of maturity it has inherited. Some religious leaders have taught that spiritual longing is a desire to rest in the power of a supernatural God, instead of a longing to fulfill the urges of the natural human potential for spiritual maturity.

The conditional factor in fulfilling potentials. A potential can do nothing until a channel is provided for the flow of its energy. All

events have two causes: the "efficient cause," or
potential, which supplies the power, and the "conditional cause" which supplies the channel for the
flow of power.

When we spill a cup of water the upset cup
provides the channel or "condition" for the fall
of the water; the gravitational potential is the
"efficient cause" for the fall.

When we turn on an electric light we provide
the circuit, or conditional cause, for the light;
the electrical potential is the efficient cause;
turning the switch would not produce light if
there were no electrical potential in the wires.

If the roof leaks we can do nothing about the
gravitational potential which brings the water in;
we have to attend to the condition of the roof.

When it was discovered that billions of
chance conditions were required to produce human
intelligence, it was thought that intelligence was
produced wholly by chance, ignoring the potential.
Yet one could take chances on a pin-ball machine
forever and it would never produce a person because such machines do not have the potential for
producing persons.

If energy had not had the potential for operating intelligently, as it does in our heads, the
mind could never have come into existence. Yet
the potential cannot produce things in violation
of such natural requirements as time, effort, and

mathematics. Clearly the potential has definable characteristics.

Electricity has always had the potential for operating gadgets such as television, but it had no special drive to produce television until the necessary equipment or circuits were completed. Apparently energy had no drive for human maturity until human beings were evolved. Potentials do not take the initiative in creating television, people, or anything else.

The potentials of energy are the first and uncaused cause of all that exists. In the sense that they are the creator of all people and things they fulfill one of the most common definitions of god. Yet they are indifferent to whether they produce edible or poisonous mushrooms, saints or sinners. That does not mean that they can produce everything imaginable. They cannot make your old car into a new one.

One can imagine flying to the moon on a supernatural carpet; but in order to actually do anything it is necessary to study the requirements and fulfill them. Traditional religions have thought it their duty to encourage the hope of a supernatural power that could do anything, because their religion and morality required such a God.

However, we have found that such beliefs make it almost impossible to develop and use a scientific understanding of requirements, and we are now finding that such supernatural hopes make almost impossible the understanding and development of true spirituality.

Evolution has developed in human beings a pattern of their maturity in body, mind, and spirit. Individuals strive to fulfill this pattern since it is needed for human survival. Human beings require the love and helpfulness of nurturing families. People feel a hunger or drive toward becoming the kind of mature parents that our species requires. They feel this drive as a longing for love and responsibility, but when these inner desires are interpreted as the voice of a separate God, it is logical to suppose that they reveal absolute truth, and provide invincible aid.

Such suppositions create arrogance, false hopes and resistance to new knowledge or improvements. The biblical view of God waiting patiently for the door of the heart to be opened (Rev. 4.20) is a more accurate picture of the lack of assertiveness in the potential or power, but it is false, in the naturalistic view, in picturing the power as separate, outside, conscious, and almighty.

Purpose, Choice, and Chance

Let us now consider some questions often raised about the source potential.

Purpose. Does the source, or god, have a purpose? Purpose implies a conscious goal, but since consciousness requires a developed brain for storing and relating memories, it is evident that evolution could not have any such complicated organism in the beginning. Therefore it could not start with what might be called a reason or conscious purpose.

But how about an unconscious goal-seeking, like a river being pulled to the sea? A river is a good analogy of the way potentials are directed by the channels which are available to it. But the river is moved by only one potential -- gravitation -- whereas evolution was pulled in many directions by potentials both good and bad.

People were evolved, not because the spiritual potential was stronger and pulled the evolutionary process "toward the image of the divine," but because spiritually mature people were more fit to survive, as has been shown in the advances of civilization. The things that make for survival are discovered and developed by evolving experiences with conditions on earth; they do not appear to be foreordained.

Furthermore, since our earth is the only planet which to our knowledge favors human life, it seems quite earth-centered to say that the whole universe is predisposed in our favor.

We have no guarantee of our future. We will surely die. Our world will some day be destroyed. We have only a limited time to make significant use of our opportunities. We have no grounds for complacency. Granted that even though we destroy our earth, probably another world of intelligent beings will eventually evolve. Yet that will be due to the chance that like conditions will appear, producing like results, rather than because of a natural predilection. The potential for life is eternal but so is the potential for death.

Since it appears that an all-wise God does not decide our goals or guarantee them, it is sometimes supposed that we are free to do as we please. But we are not free. We cannot live like brute animals and remain sane. The goal of intellectual and spiritual maturity has been bred into us. We are restless until we identify ourselves with our mature potentials. Although evolution has no goals, it has given us goals, such as survival and maturity, which we cannot escape.

Choice and chance. Traditionalists may claim that nothing happens by chance because God's purpose is being wrought in all that happens. Similarly, some scientists insist that choice and chance are impossible since the future is wholly determined by the past. Nevertheless we find that accidents can be prevented, and that people do make choices. How is freedom possible in a world of inviolable law?

Our explanation is that although all bodies give and receive influences, such as heat and gravitation, so that nothing is wholly free, yet in other respects, all bodies have a high degree of individuality.

Even an amoeba has a life-history of its own. It has a time and place of origin, it has its own position and velocity, and its experiences have imprinted upon it pulsations of energy which may take the form of rhythms, memories, or habits. Granted that there are causes for all these distinguishing marks, yet as a separate entity the amoeba's behavior reflects its unique experiences.

Likewise, people are combinations of established character and passing influences. When Jones and Smith, driving their cars, collide at an intersection, both have good reasons for being there. They are moved by causes. But Mr. Jones's line of causes was essentially independent of Mr. Smith's.

It may be that if we had known all about Jones, Smith, and the other conditions, we could have predicted the accident. Yet we still call the collision "chance," for the dictionary does not say that chance is an event contrary to the causal order, but rather that it is an occurence which was not intended or purposed. Jones and Smith did not intend to collide.

After any event it is easy enough to say that, given the conditions, the result was inevitable, but before the event it is impossible to say what conditions will be present, since at any moment an unknown, independent factor may intervene to change the result.

Granted that all factors in a decision are caused (for if they were uncaused they would be uncontrollable), yet the person responds according to the unique person he or she has become. For example, people who have less understanding of goals and consequences are more likely to be swayed by fleeting considerations, such as a chance memory, or a surge of primitive desire.

Since nothing is completely independent, the only freedom possible is the freedom to exert the mind and spirit which the individual has been caused to have. We want freedom, not from the causal order which enables us to act with predictable results, but from an environment which prevents our own causes from operating.

We are responsible for our acts, since what we are at any moment determines what we choose or how we respond.

Right Relations with the Source

We have been trying to clarify the concept of the source in order that we might develop more

meaningful and helpful relationships with it.
Most of us were taught to believe that only by
personifying god could one hope to have a spiritual experience of it.

One of Martin Buber's contributions was to
show that we can have "I--Thou" relationships with
inanimate objects. In a sense they speak to us
and we can respond to them.

We do not experience a mountain just by looking at it, but by feeling its endurance, its
majesty, its potentials, and perhaps by putting
some of our own poetry into it.

We can experience the spiritual potential in
ourselves and others by letting these potentials
guide us, and by developing an inspirational response to the potential for grandeur which we find
in all people.

The purpose of religion is not to provide
spiritual experiences, but to cultivate spiritual
growth, that is, growth in love and magnanimity.
The purpose of going to church is not to secure
relief from the annoyances of the week; the cure
for annoyance is not to supply a pacifier, the
cure is to cultivate patience and spiritual
strength.

We may need a respite from our troubles, but
to think of that as the primary reason for going
to church is like going to school not to learn,
but to get comfort for failing to learn. Reli-

gions have often been content to provide solace for those who fail.

We experience the spiritual potential, not in the hope of ecstasy, but to hear its answer when we ask, "What is the loving, the responsible, the magnanimous thing to do?" The inner voice which replies is not a supernatural authority, nor is it wholly a "superego" imposed by social pressures; it is the potential for social awareness, or spiritual maturity, contributed by the evolution of our species.

The dependability of natural law reassures us that the potential for beings who understand and care will be fulfilled whenever and wherever conditions permit. In a universe of vast spaces where there is no caring, the reassurance that there are some living specks of care may not be as comforting as is the idea of a separate, conscious spirit of love, or as the concept of personal immortality.

Yet the word "person" originally meant the mask of an actor. When a friend dies we mourn the loss of the mask, but if our primary love is for the inner spiritual potential, we will not fear death, for the person who dies is the mask of a potential for magnanimity which cannot be destroyed.

Chapter 3. THE LAWS OR REQUIREMENTS FOR LIFE

We have discussed the source of life, now let us turn to its requirements. People generally recognize that it is necessary to do certain things to repair a car, or to set a broken leg. Few people expect such work to be done for them by a supernatural power.

Nevertheless, many religious people have supposed that only the power of God could make bad men good. This opinion implies two separate and different kinds of power in the universe: on one level a natural power which requires natural energy and laws, but on a higher level, a supernatural power able to do things by command regardless of energy or the requirements of natural law.

Belief in a supernatural God who could eliminate effort was based on the ancient explanation of creation. When it was thought that God by command had created the world in a perfect condition like a Garden of Eden there was no thought of improving on primitive man. The goal of life was to get back to the original perfection, and only a supernatural God could restore the original goodness of all his works.

If the ancient biblical writers had known about the difficult evolutionary requirements for producing life, they might have surmised that spiritual developments require effort also. Since they did not realize that human beings have always needed growth and improvement, they did not look for the natural requirements of such growth.

On the campus of Columbia University there is a statue of the God of Learning. Students there do not suppose that this God can supply an education without effort; they do not worship it as a substitute for study; they do not hope to win an academic degree by acts of piety. Yet many people do worship the source of the human spirit, or God, in the hope of winning the good life by supernatural grace rather than by meeting the difficult requirements for becoming spiritually mature persons.

In an effort to overcome the supernaturalism which remains in our culture, the three sections of the present chapter will focus on (A) understanding natural requirements, (B) The unreality of the supernatural hope, and (C) The religious implication of natural requirements.

Understanding Natural Requirements

Definition of nature. Romantics have often thought of nature as kind; scientists have sometimes described it as cruel. I shall use the word as commonly employed by John Dewey and the modern school of naturalism to include everything that actually is, both good and bad, the spiritual as well as the physical.

Naturalism is like science in refusing to be content with supernatural explanations. This does not mean that it rejects spiritual explanations; people often do things for love, but it believes that love cannot cause things to happen arbitrarily, regardless of energy. For it takes the physical energy of a person to express love; love does not exist as a separate, independent force.

Nor, in the naturalistic view, does any other mind or emotion exist independently of physical bodies, or possess such almighty power that it can set aside natural requirements and do things by command. To take an obvious example, one cannot fly to the moon on a magic carpet, or by prayer; the physical requirements for getting there must be met.

Everyone recognizes some natural requirements; no one tries to live without eating or
breathing. Yet, since the Bible says that "all
things are possible," some people suppose that all
things are possible without meeting requirements.

Sometimes the requirement may be for love,
rather than for direct physical force, but love
must act through people whose loving acts obey
natural laws.

Sometimes the requirements for a goal are not
yet known, but we can always reject the supernaturalists' hope of avoiding effort by getting God
to do the work for us.

The necessity of natural requirements. It is
often difficult to prove that natural requirements
are indeed necessary. Nevertheless, some necessities may be admitted. To the extent that, or in
the way that, two plus three equals five, it is
apparent that the rule need not have been decreed
by a supernatural power who could have ordered the
sum to be eight. On the contrary, the rule is
necessary because both sides of the equation are
only different ways of saying the same thing --
two plus three ARE five.

Many laws of nature can be stated mathemati-
cally, and to the extent that the equations apply,
they are necessary. However, in more complex
activities, such as love, the requirements can

hardly be stated in mathematical terms. Are they
then supernatural?

Albert Einstein observed,

We have penetrated far less deeply
into the regularities obtaining with
the realm of living things, but deeply enough nevertheless to sense the
rule of fixed necessity... The more a
man is imbued with the ordered regularity of all events the firmer becomes his conviction that there is no
room left by the side of this ordered
regularity for causes of a different
nature... To be sure, the doctrine of
a personal God interfering with natural events could never be refuted
in the real sense, by science, for
this doctrine can always take refuge
in those domains in which scientific
knowledge has not yet been able to
set foot. But I am persuaded that
such behavior on the part of the
representatives of religion would not
only be unworthy but fatal. For a
doctrine which is able to maintain
itself not in a clear light but only
in the dark, will of necessity lose
its effect on mankind, with incalcul-
able harm to human progress... Teach-

ers of religion must have the stature
to give up the doctrine of a personal
God... which in the past placed such
vast power in the hands of priests.
   --Albert Einstein, "Out of My Later
Years." Philosophical Library, 1950,
p. 28 ff.

Einstein was not rejecting the idea of a
source or cause (which might be called "god");
what he did deny was that this cause was a supernatural or arbitrary power.

   The evolutionary evidence. Even when evidence for the evolutionary process became over-
whelming, many people thought that supernaturalism
could still be defended.

   But it is now clear that evolution has implications which are incompatible with supernaturalism: (a) supernaturalism supposes that creation
began with a fully developed, personal God; evolution implies that creation began with the totally
undeveloped potential for persons; (b) in the
supernaturalistic view the creative power is,
generally, a distinct entity separate from, and
wholly other than, the people and things created;
evolution implies that the creative power is within what is created; it is not a separate or different power; (c) by definition a "super-natural"
creator is not limited by nature; evolution shows

that the process was limited by natural requirements.

Furthermore, it seems inconceivable that a
God believed to heal the suffering of an individual would have permitted the long, cruel process
of evolution to go on for millions of years if it
were possible to set these natural requirements
aside and move directly and humanely toward the
creation of spiritually mature people.

Faith may be supported by coincidence, but a
few fortunate events can never make up for all the
brutality and indifference suffered in the past.
Evolution is an emphatic statement of the necessity for natural requirements.

Supernaturalists' Arguments

The moral defense. Supernaturalists have
argued that fear of supernatural punishment is
needed to make bad men good, restrain tyrants, and
promote righteousness. Certainly this view is
hallowed by tradition. Yet so good a theologian
as Paul Tillich argued that supernaturalism has
exactly the opposite effect. Belief in a God who
will eventually set everything right has encouraged irresponsibility; belief in God-chosen kings,
clergy, and husbands has produced most of the
tyranny from which humanity has suffered; belief
that successes prove divine favor has made nations

and individuals arrogant and ruthless; the hope of supernatural reward has caused people to waste their lives in rituals.

People are still killing each other in Ireland, India, Palestine and elsewhere because they think that God has given them supernatural rights. To be sure, the power and authority of the church have been strengthened by supernaturalistic beliefs, but strengthening the church has weakened the maturity of the people.

It has been argued that, although naturalism may satisfy the sophisticated, immature people need mythological Gods. But that was the argument for worshipping the golden calf: simple people needed a visible God. We do not close our high schools when we find that some people are not ready for them. It is the business of religion to prepare people for a mature spirit.

Examining the evidence. Supernaturalists often give reports of healing by faith, talking with the dead, clairvoyance, or mental telepathy as evidence that supernatural events do happen. My own investigations as well as those of many scientists have not substantiated those claims.

To be sure, people are sometimes healed by faith, but it seems more likely that confidence, by relaxing worries, may release healing forces within the body, rather than that faith has brought in supernatural help. People are often saved from danger but statistics do not support the claim that faith increases the likelihood of rescue.

An Episcopalian chaplain in the Second World War created a furor by pointing out that devout and righteous aviators were just as likely to be lost on dangerous missions as the irreligious.

At times the arrival of birds has provided food for starving people; a wave has sometimes saved a person by washing him ashore. But since more people are lost at sea than are saved by such coincidences, the rescues hardly prove supernatural care; what would be argued if the good people who were not rescued could tell their story?

Granted that the Earth would not be inhabited if it did not provide conditions generally favorable to human life, yet there is no guarantee that these favorable conditions will continue.

Most of us have experienced coincidences which could be offered as proof of supernatural care. A chance meeting with my sister at the end of a difficult and anxious trip was only one of many events that I might call "providential;" they led me to spend many years investigating "spirit" phenomena. But eventually I realized that attention given to these experiences, instead of helping me spiritually, was producing the Pharisaical attitude of supposing that I was especially chosen of God, when I might equally point to my misfortunes as proof that I was especially cursed.

One of the most decisive counts against the supernaturalistic view is that it implies an unjust or arbitrary selection of people for favors and hardships.

What for me was even worse was the realization that the time spent in these studies was doing nothing either to advance knowledge, or to strengthen the spirit of love, understanding, and responsibility which would make life better. Like Rubik's cube, the study was an amusing challenge, but not a constructive use of time.

The popularity of astrology and fundamentalism may indicate widespread dissatisfaction with mainstream religion, but it is doing nothing to improve spiritual maturity. Time spent on these studies is an evasion of religious responsibilities.

Devotees may claim that they are increasing our knowledge of the "spirit." But they mean by "spirit" only a separate, supernatural spirit who supposedly supplies perfect knowledge which must be stubbornly defended, rather than the spirit of conciliation, understanding, and love.

Surely the triumphs of the Greeks and Romans in government, art, philosophy, and human refinement, gave them reason to suppose that they, rather than the Jews, were the chosen people.

Monotheism may have been a modest advance over polytheism, but the main handicaps of animistic superstition were still present in Christian supernaturalism.

When Jesus warned against building one's house on the sand, he surely had in mind the danger of building upon John the Baptist's false hope of supernatural help in liberating the nation from Rome. His warning is equally applicable to the danger of building one's religion on the hope of gaining spirituality by arbitrary formulas, rather than by striving for spiritual growth.

Some supernaturalists have been elated by reports that people whose hearts have stopped beating experienced a calm before being restored to life. But clearly the brains of these people had not died; they were calm after giving up the struggle. Only those with an inordinate eagerness for evidence of the supernatural would regard such peace as proof that these people had gone to heaven and returned.

The supernaturalism in Plato's idealism. Plato argued that creation began with an idea. Certainly anything a person makes starts with an idea. However, Plato thought that memories could be stored without any equipment for storing them; ideas could be produced without any means for relating various concepts.

Evolution suggests that creation began with a totally undeveloped but necessary potential. It was like an electrical potential awaiting a circuit to lead it into action not chosen by the electricity.

All theories of creation begin with some necessary or uncreated power. It is remarkable that this power or energy has the potential for producing television pictures, as it does when supplied with television equipment, or for working intelligently, as it does when a human brain has evolved.

The equipment for fulfilling any potential must be supplied by factors or conditions outside the potential. To suppose that the universe started with an idea is like supposing that it started with a fully developed and experienced mind.

Supernaturalists sometimes charge that natural explanations stifle imagination. But imagination is not a substitute for reality. Science and mathematics supply the rules which make possible a more effective use of imagination.

Wishful supernaturalism. The primary basis for belief in supernaturalism is not reason but the wish to have a God who guarantees our care on earth, and a better life after death. But does anyone really wish to believe that his difficult responsibilities are mere make-work assignments given by a God who could easily eliminate the tasks? The person whose goal is spiritual maturity has no occasion to build his life and religion around such occult speculations.

Supernaturalism is an attempt to do without natural causes; it does not really make events more spiritual since spirituality is the introduction of the power of the spirit, not the elimination of physical effort. But couldn't a person believe in the supernatural and still be committed to the power of love?

It is probable that one could, but if one believes in the supernatural he presumes that he does not need any other help, and it is presumptuous to seek it. The warrior and the swindler need the supernatural hope, because they, of all people, realize the weakness of the brute. On the other hand, one cannot have much faith in the power of love and democracy if his main commitment is to a supernatural power.

Since in the past supernaturalism has been considered the source and center of spirituality, it is rather startling to discover that in fact the opposite is true; faith in the supernatural is destructive of faith in the spirit, but supernaturalism is an important adjunct of trust in brute force.

Mystical Requirements

Evelyn Underhill, an authority on mysticism, defines it as "the science of union with the absolute (E. Underhill, "Mysticism," Meridian, 1950, p. 72). Perhaps we may understand "the absolute" to mean the absolutely uncaused cause, the basic reality which underlies or supports all other realities.

Those who think of this reality as supernatural will interpret mystical union with it as something arbitrary, magical, and mysterious; those of us who see the absolute as natural find unity with it in accepting the requirements of life. The central task of religion is to help subordinate brute survival drives in order to unify life around the impetus for mature humanity.

Human maturity can be fulfilled only at considerable sacrifice of the pleasures associated with efforts toward physical survival, such as eating and mating.

Our wills are dominated by the physical survival drives which originated at the very beginning of organic life. The drive for spiritual maturity is much more recent; its pleasures seem relatively tame. Although the spiritual traits which distinguish human maturity are necessary for the survival of humanhood, we are much less aware of our need to express them.

In order to build mature human life we have to relax the physical survival bonds which mark the infant and the brute, and learn to identify ourselves with the spiritual potentials which are the source and goal of humanity.

I have no objection to calling this unity with the reality of our being "mysticism," and I trust that traditional mystics have no objection either. Horace Alexander, a distinguished mystical friend of Gandhi, says:

> Whenever a person surrenders to an inner prompting of spontaneous generosity, that man or woman is undergoing a mystical experience... ("Then And Now," Anna Brinton, editor, Univ. of Pennsylvania Press, 1960, p. 304.)

If a person is at one with the ultimate potential for love and responsibility, he or she is acting in loving and responsible ways, not thinking what an ecstatic feeling he/she has.

No doubt absolute unity with one's real goals provides supreme satisfaction, but when we think of it as an arbitrary gift bestowed on a few saints because of their piety, we cut ourselves off from the spiritual maturity which is the essence of mysticism. The spiritual potential is "absolute." We do not create it; but we do have to create the conditions in ourselves for its fulfillment.

Aldous Huxley called mysticism "The Perennial Philosophy." Indeed, the longing to transcend brute living is perennial. However, mysticism is sometimes thought to be the perennial wish to escape reality by hoping for supernatural solutions. We forget that our world is not the center of the universe, that we were not arbitrarily chosen for bliss.

The life-giving source is a potential which can do nothing until a channel is provided for its fulfillment. Unless we remake ourselves into circuits through which the potential for mature living can flow, our spiritual potential will remain as unrealized as the television potential, or electricity, without a television set.

The fact that Rufus Jones and Thomas Merton were influential mystics had little to do with the circumstance that one was a Quaker and the other a Catholic. Both were men of exceptional ability. We will produce more people like them, not by making more Catholics, Quakers, or Zen Buddhists, but by freeing our culture from the handicaps which hinder spiritual growth.

One does not need to be an artist, a clergyman, a Christian or Hindu. What one does need is to have what Edward Carpenter called "the whole look of himself in his eyes," the look of unity with reality which comes when selfishness and superstition are weeded out, and the real human life of spiritual maturity has been rooted in.

The Challenge. The unity and strength of spirit implied in "mysticism" does not come from the mysterious and unknown, but from facing reality.

> The more we learn of the nature of man and of the universe which gives him lodging, the more evident it becomes that his business on this planet is difficult. Everything of value the human race has achieved has taxed his resources to the uttermost. To detach himself from his brute ancestors, to invent his earliest tools, to lay the rough foundations of civilized life and then to carry it on to the point it has now reached -- these represent titanic achievements, which only a race of heroic fiber could have accomplished. What all this has cost in suffering, in courage, in endurance, in ingenuity, in patient wisdom, baffles the imagination.
>
> There is a dream of life in which the last straw of difficulty has been lifted, the last peril extinguished,

the last lee-shore weathered and all smooth sailing forever afterwards. May it never come true! Man is not made to live under those conditions. It is precisely when his circumstances are easiest that he gives the poorest account of himself, and the best when he is fighting against odds.

Both in his mind and in his body man is adapted for enterprises of great pith and moment, for dangerous expeditions into the unknown, for stern and anxious battles with the powers of darkness, for standing up to tremendous shocks, for enduring heartbreaking reverses, and for rising up when he has been wounded and beaten to the ground. To a being so splendidly equipped it is no cause for whining when he finds himself upon "an engagement very difficult."
--L. P. Jacks, "The Challenge of Life," Hodder & Stoughton, 1924. Reprinted by permission.

The dream of "smooth sailing forever afterwards" has attracted millions to traditional religion, and it has claimed to enrich the human spirit. But true courage is not based upon false hopes; true generosity does not require assurances of reward. Faith in a supernatural spirit may enable martyrs to be unswerving, but it weakens the attitude needed to find solutions.

Mystical unity with the spirit is not manifested by belief in the supernatural, but rather by the actual exercise of the magnanimous spirit.

Barbarians are again destroying our cities. Great courage is required of all of us. If we are to remain human we must accept the requirements of a mature life and develop institutions for cultivating the human spirit as untrammelled by supernatural hopes as are our great universities.

Chapter 4. THE GOALS OF LIFE

I wake up at dawn eager for the sunshine, and for the fresh morning air. It is like a new birth, for we all give a cry -- a cry for life -- with our first breath.

Yet, though we waken so eagerly, we often come to the end of the day disappointed. Where is the life for which we were crying? Did our brute ancestors lead us astray by giving us impulses that no longer belong to us as human beings? Were we misled by deceptive attractions, or by false religious hopes? What was it we really wanted?

Stages in the Development of Human Goals

1. **Survival.** Let us begin by observing how goals develop. The first objective of brute animals, as well as of human infants, is survival.

All organisms have to make an effort to get the food, sex, and power they need for self-preservation. Animals and infants give practically all their attention to their survival needs. They have little time or capacity for anything else. We inherit such strong drives for survival, and such pleasure in fulfilling them, that it is difficult to be conscious of any other purpose.

Some people think they would be content with a life which offers nothing more than eating and mating. Poets have often praised the joys of mere existence. Scientists have sometimes concluded that physical survival is the only good, since any other goal might save the unfit and cause degeneration.

Primitive religion was concerned primarily with warding off bodily harm, and even today, eternal survival is the religious goal of many people.

2. **Obedience.** As one grows from infancy to childhood, or as groups advance from sub-human to primitive social life, obedience becomes paramount. Children are forced away from their own pleasures and are required to meet the demands of their elders. They learn a language and have to follow its rules. They come under the authority of the family, school, church and community.

At an early age they learn that "what is good for them" is not what they want, but what others force upon them by their rewards and punishments. We may try to resist, but human life requires that we live in society and we never escape its authority.

Adults often continue to stress the need for authority; it eliminates uncertainty and gives strength to one's church or nation. Nevertheless, we see that the obedience which Russian peasants have given to their Czars and Commissars has been "childish;" if they had been mature enough to accept their own responsibilities they need not have remained in poverty and terror. Many Moslems are similarly handicapped.

It is more difficult to see our own weaknesses, yet we are aware of a difference in spiritual strength between those Protestants and Catholics who insist on obedience to the church, the Bible, or to God, and those who accept personal responsibility.

When as a young man I was applying for a passport to Singapore, the clerk, who was a retired missionary, looked at me closely and said, "You can tell now what you will be like twenty years from now. Many people in religious work become increasingly narrow, uncompromising, backward-looking, and mean-spirited. Others become more understanding, broader in sympathies and greater in love. You can't avoid difficulties, but you can decide now whether your ideal is obedience or magnanimity."

Later, when the neo-orthodox theologians began demanding conformity to their ideas of God, it was clear that they were being lured by the power of a religion which demands obedience. Before accepting that road, let us consider two other goals.

3. **Freedom.** As we move from childhood to adolescence, or as society moves from feudalism to democracy, people react against authority and turn to freedom as their main objective. Individually this period of revolt seldom lasts long, since young people are normally eager for responsibilities, but our society still accepts the myths of this adolescent stage in human development. "Free world," "free life-styles," "free enterprise," are popular slogans.

Many people regard freedom as the ultimate goal and test all things by whether they promote or restrict freedom. Granted that freedom may be a tool needed to reach our goals, just as a hammer may be needed to build a house, yet the goal is not to get a hammer. Freedom is of value only if it is used to build a significant and satisfying life.

We are living at a time when many new freedoms are being enjoyed by both men and women. It is easy to see how other races or groups handicap

themselves by emphasizing their freedoms rather
than enriching their life by making use of their
opportunities, but it is more difficult to see our
own failings.

After the Second World War the Japanese might
have spent their time resenting their new limitations; instead they profited greatly by capital-
izing on their new opportunities. It will help us
all if we fix our minds upon a goal beyond freedom.

4. **The final goal: maturity in body, mind,
and spirit.** As we grow in experience, we find
that life's final goal is to fulfill its potentials: to become mature in body, mind, and spirit.

Even a child may have a mature spirit if it
fulfills its childhood potential for understanding
and responsibility. But if the child does not
grow in such concerns, we soon find that it is no
longer maturing, because its spirit has not kept
up with its enlarging potentials.

A mature person is one who acknowledges and
respects other people, and who encourages human
responses from them. This is also known as the
democratic spirit, for spirituality is a social
concern.

Since growth is unconscious, we might suppose
that this goal does not require attention. It is
true that much of our physical growth does not
require thought, and even growth in mind and spir-

it is part of a process which is as insistent as an apple tree maturing its fruit.

Nevertheless, the development of our minds does need the aid of schools, and we have found it equally important to have religious institutions to help in the difficult task of cultivating the human spirit -- the intangible capacities of human life such as the feelings of love and responsibility. It is these social or spiritual potentials which stimulate us to become more than animals struggling to stay alive, and instead to become magnanimous human beings.

If our vast universe were existing without anyone's being aware of it or caring for it, how could it be said to have any value? It would make no difference if it ceased to be. The need and the capacity to understand and care are the basis of all values, and are therefore of supreme worth. Even the capacity to evolve the universe is no more important than the human capacity to appreciate it.

People sometimes claim personal satisfaction as the ultimate goal of life and religion. Granted that satisfaction is an inherited mechanism needed to point us toward activities required for survival, nevertheless it is clear that our satisfactions often misguide us.

For example, Hindus often claim great spiritual satisfaction or exaltation from walking

through fire, or performing other rituals of self-
torture. Most westerners would want to see whether fire-walkers become spiritually more mature,
or whether such physical shocks prevent devotees
from fulfilling their spiritual potentials.

Similar exaltations often reward those who
practice Christian rituals. Are these satisfactions derived from the fulfillment of spiritual
potentials, or does the bliss come from a mistaken
sense of virtue? It appears to me that supernaturalistic ideas stifle the very exercises of
mind and spirit which give life significance.

Maturity contrasted with traditional goals

Let us see how the natural interpretation of
human goals differs from the traditional, supernaturalistic explanation. An obvious change is
that in the primitive view the world began with
the creation of a perfect garden; therefore the
goal was to return to a divinely created beginning, rather than striving for growth.

A more fundamental difference is in the concepts of effort. Ancient people knew nothing of
the high voltage needed for lightning, therefore
they thought that it struck at will. They had no
knowledge of the time and energy required for
evolution, consequently they thought God had only
to say, "Let there be a man," and a man would

appear from nowhere like Aladdin's jinni. An almighty creator could produce anything without effort. Therefore the purpose of life and religion was to worship a completed power rather than to help fulfill a developing one.

Even the existence of a completed God would have to come from potentials within, rather than being imposed by still another power from the outside.

The goal of this God would be, like our own, to fulfill his significant potentials, not to praise them. His tasks would not be artificial; they would be really necessary, just as we find ours to be.

Belief in a supernatural God is popular because such a God can promise anything, without requiring physical effort. The naturalistic view is not only more plausible, but it is also more helpful in encouraging serious effort toward spiritual maturity. Augustine's restlessness for God seems more applicable to the longing for significant goals than for a return to the comforts and dependence of childhood.

Spirituality does not mean faith that love will always succeed in obtaining its goal; that would be magic. But it does mean faith that spiritual maturity is the goal of humanness, whether or not it accomplishes its immediate purpose.

The Survival Value of Spiritual Maturity

According to evolutionary theory, biological progress is due, not to a divine plan, but to the survival of the fittest. The distinguishing characteristics of each species have developed because they were needed for the survival of that way of life. Turtles need a hard shell because they are slow. But how do the spiritual characteristics which distinguish human beings aid their survival?

Some people have claimed that compassion and other spiritual qualities detract from survival strength; therefore, they suggest that spirituality must be a supernatural gift. However, since science is not satisfied with supernatural explanations, we must try to see how spiritual developments do aid survival.

Human motherhood has evolved to supply the need of human infants for greater and longer care. The pattern of spiritual maturity has developed to supply the need among humans for strong social relationships. Languages are constructed and learned in families or communities where there is a large amount of mutual understanding, sympathy, and trust. We could live as brute animals, without these advantages, but in evolving a human manner of living we could not survive without developing these spiritual qualities. Thus spirituality is not only an ideal goal for humanity; it is necessary for survival.

Why Spirituality is Needed

Democracy cannot succeed where people have stagnant minds or immature spirits. Modern tools and weapons are too dangerous to be in the hands of those who are brutish or childish. Yet our institutions for cultivating the spirit often retain the primitive view that spirituality is a matter of communicating with a supernatural God.

We must learn to recognize democracy as at the heart of spirituality. The need for spiritually mature people may force as great changes in religion during the next thirty years as we have had in the thirty centuries since Western religion advanced from voodoo worship.

In horse-and-buggy days, wheels wobbled as they meandered along country roads. Today, if wheels are not mounted with precision, the vehicle is a menace. The destructive power of automobiles is so great that if people are to travel safely, adequate equipment must be developed and maintained.

A similar fulfillment of the highest standards of spiritual maturity has become imperative. Without proper wheels we are not free to drive cars; without spiritually mature people we cannot have a creative or democratic society.

Although our spiritual capacities are like the physical in being necessary for the survival of the species, we should remember the differences. The needs for physical survival are physical; the survival of humanness requires the development of intangible or spiritual qualities such as love, justice, understanding and appreciation. We cannot eliminate physical needs, but we can keep them from enslaving us to a brute existence.

The conflict between physical and spiritual goals is not an inheritance from "Adam's sin;" instead it is one of the difficult struggles in our evolution from brute to human, or in our growth from infancy to maturity.

Our ancestors from the beginning of organic life have had to do the things necessary for physical survival. As a result, material needs are at the forefront of consciousness, often crowding out awareness of spiritual or social needs which are of more recent origin.

Furthermore, it is the family or community which suffers more obviously when a person fails to mature spiritually; the failure of humanness brings no physical pangs of hunger or of suffocation. The humanity of the person or the community may be destroyed, but the individual may not recognize the threat to his humanness.

With these naturalistic answers to the ultimate questions of source, duty, and goals, let us
turn now to the implications of naturalism for
that center of our Western religious tradition
which we find in the life and teachings of Jesus.

PART II

FINDING THE NATURAL JESUS

PART II

FINDING THE NATURAL JESUS

Chapter 5. GOSPEL ORIGINS

The Gospels were compiled, edited, and largely written by people who thought that Jesus was
supernatural. Since it is presumed that these
ancient writers knew more about Jesus than we do
today, it seems arrogant to attempt to reverse
their picture.

However, the Gospels give only a minority
report. Most Jews, even those who had known Jesus
personally, did not accept the New Testament Gospels.

Yet they would have followed him enthusias-
tically if he had shown the supernatural power
claimed for him in the Gospels. Instead, he met
opposition in all the synagogues and was finally
crucified, with the approval of the priests as
well as of the crowds who shouted for his death.

69

In reading the Acts of the Apostles, chapters two to four, one is struck by the fact that, except for Peter, those who started the church are not the ones who had known Jesus personally.

Scholars are particularly disturbed by finding no mention of Jesus for the first fifteen or twenty years after his death. Anything so amazing as the events reported in the Gospels would certainly have caused wide-spread comment and discussion by the leaders of Greek and Roman thought.

Yet Paul's letter to the Galatians, written about AD 47, is the earliest writing about Jesus that we have, and it is more concerned to defend Paul's personal experiences and doctrines than to tell us anything about Jesus.

For the first twenty years after his death, no one seems to have thought highly enough of Jesus to have quoted him, or offered him as an example. Apparently he really was "despised and rejected of men." (Isaiah 53).

For instance:

Classical writers of the first century are silent concerning Christianity. Tacitus, Pliny the Younger, and Suetonius, writing AD 110-120, treat Christianity as a new phenomenon which has to be explained. Of the Jewish writers, Philo does not mention the crucifixion in his critical

analysis of the career of Pontius
Pilate, which he wrote not much later
than AD 41. Josephus mentions brief-
ly John the Baptist and the martyrdom
of James in 62 but about Jesus (except in the Slavonic [Christianized]
version) he is silent.
--W. H. C. Frend, "The Early Church,"
Lippincott, 1965, condensed.

Ancient copyists often felt at liberty to
"correct" manuscripts on which they were working,
in order to bring them up to their own understanding of events.

For example, Josephus was not a Christian and
most of his manuscripts do not mention Jesus.
Therefore when we come upon a copy of Josephus
which not only mentions Jesus, but calls him
"Lord" and "God," scholars have little hesitation
in presuming that this is a "Christianized" manuscript.

We find similar "Christianizing" in the Epistle of James, in the Didache (a manuscript which
presents some of the earliest customs of the
Christian church, although with many later additions), and of course in the Gospels. For example, Eusebius, the early church historian, did not
find the trinitarian formula for baptism attached
to Matthew 28.19 in copies of the Gospel in the
fourth century.

E. G. Kraeling, in his "The Four Gospels" (McGraw Hill, 1962, p. 190) offers this explanation: "The change in the text of Matthew could have been made to provide biblical authority for the [later] ecclesiastical custom" (of baptizing in the name of the Father, the Son and the Holy Ghost).

Father Albert Nolan, A Provincial Superior of the Dominican Order, summarizes another major difference between Jesus and the Gospels:

> Jesus went to a great deal of trouble to persuade the Jews of Palestine that their present attitude of resentment and bitterness was suicidal... No assessment of the situation could have been more at variance with the expectations of the Zealots... [Said Jesus,] 'unless you change you will be destroyed.' (Luke 13.3.5.) Because they would not be able to overthrow the Romans in military battle... the only sensible thing to do was to be reconciled with them (Lk 12.58). As Jesus saw it, the only way to be liberated from your enemies was to love your enemies (Lk 6.27f). -- Albert Nolan, "Jesus Before Christianity," Orbis, Maryknoll, NY, 1978, pp 94ff.

While the "Zealots" planned destruction, and the pious Messianists hoped that God would do the destroying, Jesus saw that what was needed was the spiritual growth which would enable the Jews to accept the Romans as human beings like themselves, with whom they could work in loving cooperation.

Another Catholic scholar, Hans Kung, supports the view of a radical difference between Jesus and the Gospels. In a lecture at Harvard, Dr. Kung called for reconciliation with Islam, basing his plea on the grounds that Muhammad was following the view of the people who had actually known Jesus:

> Muhammad himself acts as a witness to Jesus, albeit not to a Jesus as Hellenistic Gentile [Gospel] Christians could have viewed him, but a Jesus as viewed by his first disciples who were Jews like Jesus himself. -- Hans Kung; reprinted by permission from Harvard Divinity Bulletin, Vol. 15/#8 (1985), pp 4-8.

Three early opposing views of Jesus

(1) The first view was that of the Essene Church in Jerusalem. We have no evidence that the people who knew and heard Jesus reported anything about him. Some scholars point out that if the

miracles had happened, we would have had earlier
and wider reports.

But when the Essene church in Jerusalem,
after Stephen's vision and stoning, adopted Jesus
as their Messiah, an effort was made (recorded in
the Didache) to follow Jesus' teaching of love
toward enemies.

The church in Jerusalem was started by a
group of people who held all things in common,
awaiting the arrival of the Messiah whom John the
Baptist had taught them to expect at any moment.
Probably they were already members of the communal
group of Essenes, or pious ones, who formed one of
the congregations of expectant Messianists which
existed in Palestine from about 168 BC until the
destruction of the city and state in AD 70. They
are the ones who produced the Dead Sea Scrolls
discovered in 1947.

These Essenes, or pious people, paid no attention to Jesus during his life. He opposed
their supernaturalistic hopes and their strict
observances. There was not the slightest reason
for them to suppose that Jesus was the Messiah
they expected to appear out of the sky with an
army to overthrow the Roman Empire and reestablish
the throne of David.

The priests were hostile to the Essenes because these pious people demanded poverty. Consequently the priests were happy to taunt them with

the failure of their Messiah to appear. The pious ones responded with denunciation of the priests for their lack of spirituality. When, instead of the arrival of a Messiah, John the Baptist himself was beheaded, the Essenes were forced to admit that something was wrong. One of the Essenes, Stephen, accused the priests of foiling God's plan by killing the prophets.

The priests responded by charging Stephen with blasphemy, and sentencing him to death by stoning. Before Stephen died, he tried to prove his charge against the priests by claiming a vision of Jesus in heaven as a Son of God (Acts 7.55ff). Stephen's dying vision further incensed the priests, but it convinced the Essenes in Jerusalem that Jesus was indeed the Messiah.

The literature of these Jewish Christians was largely destroyed. I know of only two important fragments: (a) the disciplines in Q, which I discuss on pp 78, and (b) the tract of the Essenes now called the Didache, discussed in the next four paragraphs.

This tract was discovered in 1873, and is now available in C. C. Richardson's "Early Christian Fathers," (Westminster, and also Macmillan, 1970, pp. 161-179). The Didache must have served the same purpose as Q (see below, p. 78) for, like Q, it is a Messianistic manual of disciplines to which some teachings of Jesus have been added.

Traditionalists suppose that these teachings of Jesus are quotations from the Gospel of Matthew and therefore later than 90 BC. But since the Didache knows nothing of the miracles (in Matthew) which are given as the basis for the authority of Jesus' unpopular teachings of love toward enemies, it appears that the Didachist had not heard of the miracles, and did not regard Jesus as an authority worth mentioning. The teachings in the Didache would seem not to have been copied from another manuscript but to have been received orally.

Bible students have not been prepared to believe that the early church knew nothing of the miracles, because they are told in Acts that Peter instituted the church, and they have supposed that Peter witnessed the miracles from the beginning.

Now it appears that the early chapters of Acts, as well as of the Gospels, are part of the supernaturalistic myth. Traditionalists have to dismiss the authority of the Didache because it contradicts their beliefs. Yet it is evident that the rituals of the Didache come from the Essenes, not the Gospels, even though the title and the trinitarian formula for baptism are second century or later. Since the rule of baptismal water wavers, it must come from the early transitional stage between Essene and Christian.

The early church in Antioch no doubt had similar rituals; the tract may have been used there, but I question whether it originated there. It seems more likely that these were the rules and teachings that Barnabus took to Antioch from Jerusalem, rather than the reverse.

(2) Paul's view: the second view of Jesus, contradicting the first, but forming the chief portions of the Gospels as we have them, is the one developed by Paul. His Epistles were written from about AD 47 for the next fifteen years. Paul was present at the execution of Stephen, and a few weeks after Stephen's vision Paul too heard a voice confirming Jesus as the Messianic Lord (Acts 9.8). Paul boasted that he knew nothing of the historical Jesus (Gal. 1.12) but he thought his own view was better.

Thus it appears that the two earliest branches of Christianity were started by people who had less historical knowledge of Jesus than we have today. Both Paul's and Stephen's visions were supernaturalistic. Paul added the belief that Jesus' death on the cross had redeemed mankind from the requirements of the Jewish law, particularly circumcision. I shall discuss Paul more fully later (p. 85).

(3) The naturalistic view of Jesus: The views of Jesus' family and friends were written down only after it became necessary to correct the visionary accounts of Stephen and Paul.

When Paul came to Jerusalem (about AD 46-7) hoping to get confirmation of his visionary view of Jesus as a liberator from the law, trouble began. James called Paul a "foolish fellow" (James 2.20) and Paul denied that James's life with Jesus gave him any superior knowledge (Gal. 2.6).

Since Paul would not recognize the authority of James's first-hand report, it was necessary to get impartial, official confirmation of James's story. Levi, the official tax collector and friend of Jesus, was chosen for the task. (Levi's common name was Matthew). His report is known as "The Logia," or words of Jesus.

Since the supernaturalistic view of Jesus has been the most popular, it has tended to crowd out Levi's naturalistic view. Therefore we are extremely fortunate in having Levi's first-hand account of the teachings fairly well preserved in the Logia section of Q.

We find Q (the early source identified by scholars), by taking the portions of Matthew and Luke which are alike but which do not come from Mark.

However, Q comes from two different sources: (a) the Logia, and (b) the Manual of the Jerusalem Messianists, or Essenes. We find a part of the Logia in Luke's report of the Sermon on the Plain (Lk 6.27-49); the Manual of rules is seen in what

Matthew has added to the sermon (Matt. 5.13-38, all of Matt. 6, and Matt. 7.6-15, 21-23). The Logia is discussed more fully on page 91.

"Demythologizing" the Gospels

Scholars have attempted many different methods for reconciling Gospel "miracles" with the necessary requirements of nature. Some have tried to solve the problem by calling anything that is wonderful, such as a child or a flower, "a miracle." But the purpose of the miracle stories was to prove that Jesus had powers beyond nature. If the supernatural aspects are removed, the stories have no point.

Rudolph Bultmann suggested that we should "demythologize" the Gospels. He said that "to demythologize is to deny that the message of scripture is bound to an ancient world-view which is obsolete." (Rudolph Bultmann, "Jesus Christ and Mythology," Scribner 1958, p. 36). This meant acknowledging that the stories are fictitious but insisting that the supernatural message of salvation is true. But if the supernatural is false, there must be something wrong with the message.

Thomas Jefferson supposed that to recover the historical Jesus all he had to do was to take scissors and cut the miracles out of the Gospels. Since Jefferson's day, scholars have found that

Gospel authors had created a wide assortment of other "myths" to support Paul's supernaturalistic picture of Jesus. The Nativity in Bethlehem, the Triumphal Entry into Jerusalem, the Empty Tomb, are but three of the most obvious stories required to support the legend. When all of these myths are subtracted, almost nothing is left but the Logia and some parables.

Supernaturalists believe that the core of the Gospels is not the spiritual teaching of the Logia, but the promise of a supernaturally transformed world. Apparently the fact that supernaturalistic hopes have proven false in the past does not deter them from having such hopes for the future.

> It was in this conception of thorough-going eschatology [a supernaturalistic promise] that Albert Schweitzer supposed he had found the heart of the message of Jesus... quite incorrectly, we believe... It is not so much Jesus as the faith of the primitive community which comes before us here. -- Bultmann and Kundsin, "Form Criticism," Harper, 1962, p. 100.

Today, "accepting Jesus" means being converted to piety and the church, but to the first Christians in Jerusalem, "conversion" had no such

meaning. They had been baptized into the Messianistic (or Christian) church even before they had
heard of Jesus; they were already pious people who
had surrendered everything for the Messiah. When
they accepted Jesus, they did not ask what he had
taught. They were interested only in identifying
him with their hopes.

The background of Messianism

After the conquests of Alexander (333-323 BC)
the Greeks ruled Palestine for nearly two hundred
years. When the Greek ruler in 168 BC tried to
abolish the worship of Jehovah, the Jews responded
in three ways: (a) the Maccabees rose up to save
the nation militarily; (b) the Pharisees thought
that salvation lay in stressing obedience to the
Mosaic laws, and (c) the most fanatical believed
that God would restore Palestine to the Jews
through a supernatural savior or Messiah if the
people were sufficiently pious.

This last group, often called the Essenes, or
"pious ones," built the monastery now famous as
the source of the Dead Sea Scrolls. I shall be
calling these people "Messianists" since it was
their supernatural Messianism which evolved into
the Christian faith.

When the Romans drove out the Greeks in 63
BC, the Jews cooperated gladly at first because

Roman culture and religion seemed less threatening than the Greek. Accommodation with the Romans was possible. But Jewish fanatics persisted in resistance.

A situation developed similar to that in France during the Nazi occupation. Terroristic attacks upon the Romans were ruthlessly suppressed. Resentment increased, and the struggle intensified to the holocaust of AD 70. At the time of Jesus (ca. AD 30) this conflict was reaching a climax.

In the midst of this tense situation, a "pious one" named John the Baptist (ca. AD 28) began to declare that God was ready to send his Messiah to destroy the Romans with fire and set up a kingdom on earth ruled by Jehovah and his chosen people.

Of course John's preaching received wild acclaim in Palestine. His dream was false; there was no destruction of Rome, nor rescue of the Jews. The only effect of his teaching was to embolden the freedom fighters, who made matters worse.

Thus John's Messianic prophecies were not only false, they were dangerous; they were fanning the flames of fanatical resistance which the Romans would not tolerate. Jesus did not need supernatural vision to see that revolt was suicidal. All impartial people of the Mediterranean world knew it. The kind of Messiah needed was not one who would bring more fire, but one who would bring love and reconciliation.

The Dead Sea Scrolls tell us something about the pious and self-sacrificing people who were being attracted to Messianism in Jesus' day, not because they knew anything about Jesus, but by the hope of supernatural liberation from Rome.

Mark's family is an example. The Messianists in Jerusalem met in his home. His uncle Barnabus sold land and gave the proceeds to the group (Acts 4.36ff). Yet neither Mark, Barnabus, nor any other of these Messianists is credited with having any firsthand knowledge of Jesus, although they were seeking the Messiah earnestly at the time of Jesus' supposed triumphal entry into their city.

The Dead Sea Scrolls were being written at the time of Jesus, in a monastery of the Messianists twenty miles from Jerusalem, with pilgrims and supplies going betweeen the two centers constantly. Yet, in all their ancient scrolls, Jesus is never mentioned. Apparently there was nothing about Jesus to make the Messianists suppose that he was their Messiah.

How is it then that about ten years after his death, supernaturalistic stories supporting his messiahship began to appear? This is a mystery which scholars have just begun to unravel. The stories were created to support the messianic

theories which the visions of Stephen and Paul had
stimulated.

But Jesus had had three reasons for rejecting
John the Baptist's hope of supernatural deliverance. (1) In actual practice, Jesus knew that
prayers will not make a beam strong. The requirements for sound carpentry have to be met. (2)
God's impartiality in supplying sun and rain to
all his children made divine favoritism impossible. (3) The terrorism sometimes used against
the Romans, which seemed virtuous and brave to the
Jews, were really acts which disqualified them
from God's favor.

Such views were not only in opposition to
popular hopes, they seemed treasonous. No wonder
Jesus was despised and rejected.

The book of Acts gives a whole chapter to
Stephen's martyrdom. Stephen had been dismayed
when, instead of seeing the world transformed as
John the Baptist had predicted, John himself was
beheaded. What had gone wrong?

Stephen was suspicious of the priests; they
were hostile to the Messianists for expecting
everyone to practice austerities. The Old Testament had repeatedly found the priests guilty of
failing God's plans. What innocent man had the
priests killed now? Jesus was closer to Isaiah's
vision of a despised redeemer than anyone else.
Stephen convinced himself that the priests were

indeed to blame, and began to blame them in public for killing God's messenger.

It is clear from the report of the trial that Stephen was not condemned for being a follower of Jesus, but for accusing the priests of responsibility for delaying the appearance of the Messiah. At the end of the trial Stephen, as proof of his charges, claimed to have a vision of Jesus in heaven as God's favorite.

The Jerusalem Messianists were greatly excited by Stephen's dying vision. From that day until the city was destroyed thirty-five years later, they continued to insist that Jesus was the Messiah.

Paul

Stephen's vision also had a profound effect upon Paul, who was present at the stoning. Although Paul was a Jew, he had been reared in Tarsus, a university city in Asia Minor. Alexander's followers had granted the Jews of Tarsus equal status with the Greeks, while Mark Anthony had granted Roman citizenship to all its people.

Thus Paul, like all children of Tarsus, was proud of his Roman citizenship. Paul wanted to convert his Roman friends to the worship of the one true God. He had no difficulty in persuading them of the superiority of a single just God, but his friends were adamant in regarding the Jewish initiation rite of circumcision as a vulgar superstition.

Paul wanted to be proud of his religion as well as of his citizenship. He had seen the enthusiasm generated by the Mithraic ritual of redemption through the blood of a slain bull; why couldn't Isaiah's prophecy of redemption through the blood of a slain lamb, or Messiah, be just as potent as the blood of an ox? (Isaiah 53.7, 10, 12). Why couldn't Judaism be introduced with a ritual which would inspire enthusiasm, rather than hostility?

When Paul came to Jerusalem as a young man to study religion, he was antagonized by the Messianists, not because they followed Jesus -- they paid no attention to Jesus -- but because their hostility to Rome was making conversion of the Romans more difficult. As as result, Paul became a leader in harassing the Messianists. If Stephen's haunting vision of the murdered Jesus as the Son of God were correct, then his blood shed on the cross would have the redeeming effect Paul thought was needed to overcome the requirement of circumcision.

At first it seemed impossible. But as Paul's qualms about his own responsibility for the death of Stephen increased, he was overwhelmed by the conviction that Jesus was the Messiah prophesied

by the Baptist.   On the road to Damascus to further persecute the Messianists, he was struck by
an idea which confirmed his new theories.

Probably few people today believe that God
had to crucify his own son in order to get rid of
the requirement of circumcision. But for Paul,
this theory dominated the rest of his life.

Paul's idea was bad, not only because of what
it did to the idea of God, but also because of
what it has done to the concept of religion. It
has fastened the hope of supernatural redemption
on the religion of Jesus, who had preached exactly
the opposite. It has made Christianity hostile to
other ideas, instead of encouraging the spirit of
respect, love, and conciliation which Jesus
preached; it has promoted an inflexible spirit
which Jesus opposed.

Obviously a religion which preaches its own
perfection cannot do much to build the spirit or
world we need and want. Nevertheless the idea of
winning eternal bliss through another's blood,
which had proved so successful in Mithraism, now
became equally effective in winning converts to
Paul's new doctrines.

The Jews rejected Paul's dream, but those who
knew nothing about Jesus found it easy to specu-
late that he was their savior, that he must have
been born in Bethlehem as had been prophesied, and

that the other beliefs needed to sustain their hopes were well founded.

At first Paul stood alone. As he says in Galatians (1.11), he got his ideas about Jesus from no one; they were his own inspiration. He believed that divine truth had been revealed to him, and no one was going to tell him anything. It is that bigoted attitude which makes growth of the democratic spirit almost impossible.

Paul and the eschatology of Mark may satisfy Barth's supernaturalists, but those who see with Bultmann that supernaturalism is obsolete will need to develop the naturalistic foundations for religion.

In the next chapter we shall see the great strides toward naturalism made by Jesus, due to the disastrous political situation which forced him to find better foundations for life than the supernaturalistic hope.

Chapter 6. THE TEACHINGS OF JESUS

The "L" Source

Although the Epistles of Paul, written AD 47-
62, may be our earliest completed writings about
Jesus, we do have fragments which appear to be
earlier. For example, Professor Frederick Grant
characterizes some of the material which only Luke
presents (and is therefore called "L") as follows:

> The picture we derive from L is not that
> of the transcendent "Son of Man"...
> gathering together a group who were to
> be his faithful followers... There is
> not the slightest trace of Pauline in-
> fluence upon it. Nor is there any trace
> of the institutionalism so apparent
> later... The apocalyptic-eschatological
> element... is almost absent. -- F. C.

Grant, "The Gospels, Their Origin and Growth." Harper & Row, 1957, p. 62ff.

Dr. Grant's description gives us some criteria for identifying other early sources: (a) no transcendent Jesus, (b) no followers, (c) no Pauline influence, (d) no church discipline, and (e) no eschatology.

Luke made a diligent search for the facts about Jesus, but the only personal friend of Jesus with whom Luke reports an extended visit is Philip in Samaria (Acts 21.8ff). Harnack and other scholars believe Philip to be the chief source of the L material, particularly since the L parables have had their political meaning removed to provide bed-time stories for Philip's four daughters.

Nevertheless the original political purpose of the stories is still discernible. "The Good Samaritan" must have been "The Good Roman." Scholars have noticed that the use of a Samaritan in the story is evidence that the parable had been adapted for Philip's use in Samaria.

The Prodigal Son (Lk 15.12-32) was even more central to Jesus' political message. The story was told to suggest that the wayward son (the Romans) had God's love as much as did the more faithful son (the Jews). How that story must have infuriated those to whom Jesus first told the parable! The idea of equality before God destroyed what was then the Jews' most cherished religious belief: the conviction that they were God's chosen people.

Jesus' teaching of equality caused so much bitterness that Luke did not venture to refer to it again, and Matthew deals with it only in Jesus' observation that the sun rises equally on the evil and the good. It is generally acknowledged that these parables are authentic, for anyone could have told about the Messianistic hope, but only an innovator could have given us these unpopular observations.

The Logia

Finding the Q source. Scholars give the name "Q" to our most important Gospel source. The rule for finding Q is to take the portions of the Gospels of Matthew and Luke which the two have in common, but which do not come from Mark. We can arbitrarily say what material is included in this rule, but the rule does not define the source from which Q came.

Apparently Q has two different sources: half of the material consists of words that could have come only from Jesus because they are not like what anyone else was saying; the other half comes from rules and rituals similar to the ones we find in the Dead Sea Scrolls. Since Jesus opposed these rules he could not have formulated them.

Our knowledge of the Dead Sea Scrolls suggests that these disciplines were established long
before the Jerusalem Messianists knew anything
about Jesus. However, the Teachings of Jesus had
to be added to the disciplines as soon as the
teachings were known, because the Messianists were
now calling Jesus "Lord," even though the teachings contradict the disciplines (the Teachings
insist that prayers should be spontaneous and
private, while the disciplines write out the
"Lord's Prayer" and enjoin faithful repetition).
Since Luke's Gospel does not include the Prayer
with the authentic Sermon but puts it later (Lk
11.1ff), Luke is clearly separating the Prayer
from the teachings, further evidence that the
Prayer is not by Jesus.

The authentic teachings are separated from
the disciplines most clearly when we take the
Sermon on the Plain as it appears in Luke (6.27-
59) and then see what Matthew's Gospel (where it
is called "Sermon on the Mount") has added to it.
The additional material in Matthew chapters 5,6,
and 7 is from the disciplines of the sect. Luke
gives Jesus' words alone; Matthew mixes the words
of Jesus with the disciplines. Apparently the
compiler of Matthew's Gospel wanted to make it
appear that the rules were part of Jesus' teaching. Luke, as an opponent of Jewish disciplines,
wanted to keep them separate.

The writing of the Logia. "The Logia," or "words," is a title given to a portion of the gospels which includes "the Sermon on the Mount" and other important sayings of Jesus which appear now only in the Gospels of Matthew and Luke.

The actual writing of the Logia section of Q seems to have been occasioned by Paul's visit to Jerusalem reported in Galatians 2.1-14, at which time Paul announced his radical new theory that the blood of Jesus shed on the cross had redeemed mankind from the requirement of circumcision. This visit is usually dated about AD 45.

James then wrote his Epistle (ca. 46) denying that faith in the blood of Jesus relieved people from the requirements of the law, and calling Paul "foolish" for even suggesting it (James 2.20).

The rest of James's Epistle is a report on the religious teachings which both Jesus and James had received in their childhood home. Apparently James supposed that the mere statement of these virtues would be enough to convince Paul of their necessity, for he does not even suggest that he is quoting Jesus.

The next year Paul responded with his Epistle to the Galatians, giving his version of the Jerusalem meeting and denying that the facts given by the brother of Jesus had any authority against Paul's vision (Ga. 2.6).

Therefore James had to produce an independent, offical report of what Jesus had said. The tax collector Levi-Matthew was an official, not related to Jesus, whose position committed him to the reconciliation with Rome which Jesus advocated. He would be able to produce an official, but sympathetic, report about Jesus.

Very likely he was asked (perhaps by James) to write out the Logia, or Teachings of Jesus. At least the earliest records of the Logia report that "Matthew" was the author. No one else has been suggested as a possible author of the Logia. Jesus and Levi shared a view of the Romans which almost all other Jews rejected.

This view is contrary to the doctrines of the neo-orthodox, who must discredit the Logia because it is inconsistent with their supernaturalistic view of Jesus.

The Levi-Matthew report was incorporated into both the Gospels of Matthew and the Gospel of Luke. However, both gospels are more fully based on the Gospel of Mark.

The supernatural hope which Jesus was combating is not a trivial mistake; ten thousand Jews went unnecessarily to their death in the fall of Jerusalem, and millions of Christians since have met a similar fate because of this false hope. Most of the killing that has gone on in Ireland, Lebanon, India and two world wars has gone on under the arbitrary and uncompromising claim of divine favor. Jesus was crucified because he opposed that patriotic but unrealistic hope. Our only salvation is in establishing love, mutual respect, and the spirit of democracy.

The authority of the Logia. For nearly two thousand years the Logia, with its Sermon on the Mount (or Plain) was considered of the highest authority, because it was attributed to (Levi) Matthew, making it the only portion of the Gospels which could claim eye-witness authority. However, fifty years ago when neo-orthodox theologians began insisting that the whole purpose of the Gospels was to announce the coming of Christ's supernatural kingdom on earth, the Logia with its typical sermon by Jesus had to be thrust aside as spurious or, at best, "secular."

The more this neo-orthodox suggestion of secularism has been studied, the stronger the evidence against it has become. It is true that the canonical Matthew copies, and therefore supports, Mark's supernaturalistic report of Jesus. But when second century writers refer to "The Gospel of Matthew," they are referring to the Logia, for Gentiles didn't like Matthew's Gospel because it upheld the Mosaic Law; Jews didn't like it either because it foisted Mark's Gospel on them, which the Jews never accepted. When second century writers speak of "Matthew's Gospel" it is

clear that they usually are referring to the Logia
(Cf. Irenaeus, "Against Heresy," III, L.1;
Eusebius, "Ecclesiatical History," v 8).

The opponents of the Logia have one strong
argument: the Christians who accepted only the
Logia soon died out; the church was built by those
who were attracted by Paul's hopes. The strength
of the church today proves the power of hope to
attract followers, but it does not prove the val-
idity of such hope.

Christianity has faltered and fallen at this
point. We cannot fulfill our responsibility to
others and at the same time be indifferent to the
arduous disciplines needed for the fulfillment of
their significant potentials. Jesus could have
been popular by encouraging false hopes; he chose
instead to encourage spiritual growth.

Overview of the Logia. We now have the exciting task of uncovering the message of Jesus.
The traditional Gospels are made up largely of
random arguments and wise sayings that defend issues arising between the Messianists and Paul;
they have little to do with the teachings of
Jesus. Therefore when we come to a portion of the
Gospels which fulfills the criteria for an early
work, and at the same time presents a message
important enough for a wise man to give his life,
(and for the thoughtless to take it), we have
reason to believe that we are approaching the

authentic teachings of Jesus. We find such a message in the Logia, with its Sermon on the Mount.

Americans have seldom been in a subservient position, such as the Jews experienced at the time of Jesus. Yet in the Iranian hostage crisis of 1981 we had some similar emotions. We were suffering such indignities that those who advocated forebearance were shouted down as unpatriotic, just as Jesus had been. Few were willing to try what love could do to improve the situation.

The Text of the Logia

A. The teachings of John the Baptist. (Matt. 3, Lk 3). It was the popularity of John the Baptist's misleading and dangerous preaching which led Jesus to begin speaking out in public. One could not understand Jesus until he understood what Jesus was opposing. Therefore it was necessary to begin the account of Jesus' teaching with a reminder of John's message which might be expressed somewhat as follows:

> John the Baptist was preaching "Repent, for the kingdom of heaven is at hand. God is ready to burn up the chaff of evil." While John was still preaching at the Jordan River, Jesus

went there to hear and to be baptized
by John. -- Matt. 3.1-2.

To most Jews, John's hope that the pagans
would soon be overthrown by supernatural power
seemed reasonable because, if God had created the
world by command, he surely could save his chosen
people by command. Jesus saw no evidence that God
was more favorable to the Jews than he was to the
Romans; God loves all his children and is impartial. Therefore Jesus began to reject John's hope
of supernatural favor.

B. The Temptations. (Matt. 4.3-10) The supernaturalistic view of Jesus required the belief
that Jesus accepted, rather than rejected, John's
expectations. Therefore Mark's Gospel, and the
Gospels of Matthew and Luke, which copied from it,
had to make it appear that Jesus was tempted by
Satan, rather than by John's hope. But the character of the temptations makes it clear that Jesus
is here beginning his opposition to John's teaching. Every time Jesus warned against expecting
supernatural help, he would be challenged by people who were enthusiastic about John's promises.
Frequently Jesus would have to explain that he had
heard John preach but had rejected John's tempting
argument.

The first Temptation. (Matt. 4.3; Luke 4.3)
John's first appeal was to believe that God's
goodness demanded the destruction of paganism and

the liberation of the Jews. But Jesus knew many
good things that God does not do; he does not turn
stones into bread to feed the hungry. Therefore
Jesus concluded that God's primary concern was for
the human spirit.

The second Temptation. (Matt. 4.5ff; Lk
4.9ff). John's second appeal was his hope that if
God would show his power by destoying Rome, many
people would be led to worship the one true God.
But Jesus saw that it would also create faith if
angels would rescue people who jumped from the
pinnacle of the temple. Such people were not
rescued by angels.

The third Temptation. (Matt.4.8-10; Lk 4.5-
8). The final temptation in John's preaching was
the promise of popularity. People are so eager to
believe in supernatural benefits that they would
flock to Jesus if he would proclaim a miraculous
salvation. The Christian church has won most of
the kingdoms of the earth by offering this false
hope.

Jesus saw that it was a fiendish idea, for it
would hinder rather than encourage the spiritual
growth which people need. It would be accepting
the devil of falsehood in order to gain power.
Jesus spurned the temptation (Matt. 4.10).

C. The Sermon at Nazareth. (Lk. 4.16-21; Isa
53.3-7). After wrestling with these temptations,
Jesus went home to tell his friends that the

Baptist's hopes were false and to suggest Isaiah's spiritual Messiah as an alternative. By self-sacrifice the nation would be healed. Since the Gospel of Matthew does not report this sermon, it is technically L, but most scholars put it with the Logia because of its style and purpose.

D. The Sermon on the Mount. We now come to Jesus' central message, which in Matthew is called "The Sermon on the Mount," occupying chapters 5, 6 and 7. This long statement includes the rules of the Jerusalem church which they had derived from their experience as Essenes. Jesus opposed these rules and had nothing to do with their formulation. However, when the Jerusalem church adopted Jesus as their Messiah they had to adopt his message as well, adding the message to their rules. Thus the rules became attached to the Logia (in the version given in the Gospel of Matthew).

In Luke, the message is pictured as being given on a plain (Luke 6.27-49) and is given without the addition of the Essene rules. This must be the version as it appeared in Levi-Matthew's original Logia.

When the Logia was written (about AD 50), no one was concerned about the teachings of Jesus; not even Paul was saying anything about them. But the tax collector Levi, or Matthew, had to answer two questions: (1) Was there any basis for Paul's dismissal of circumcision? The Logia answers "No." (2) If Jesus was a good man, why was he crucified? Here the answer is equally clear: Jesus was crucified because he opposed the popular hope for supernatural liberation.

Both reports begin the sermon with a poem called "The Beatitudes," a poetic version of the opening theme from the Epistle of James. Probably Jesus often echoed the same ideas. However, the poem has nothing to do with the political sermon which follows. Let us paraphrase the message (text Lk 6.27-49) without it:

> You have heard John's promise of divine help in overthrowing Rome; now listen to me. I say that you will have to love your enemies, and do them good. If a Roman slaps you on one cheek, offer him the other also; if he robs you of your coat, give him your shirt as well; do not try to get your property back. For if you love only those who love you, how does that make you a child of God? He loves all his children equally, and is kind to the ungrateful and the wicked (Lk 6.27-36).

Objection: "But the Romans are pagans."

Answer: Why worry about the speck in your enemy's eye when you have a large block of wood in your own eye? First remove the obstruction from your own eye so that you may see how to remove the speck from your opponent's eye. A tree is known by its fruit. You are a good people, meriting God's consideration, only if you produce good fruit.

Conclusion: If you take my advice you will be like a man who built his house on good foundations. When storms came his house was unmoved, for it was founded on reality, rather than on hopes. But if you ignore my advice, you will be like a man who built his house on sand. When storms came, his house was washed away. (Lk 6.46–49)

Soon the storms did come, and Jerusalem was destroyed.

The Parables

Q contains some parables; perhaps it was the source of most of the Gospel parables. On the other hand, some of the wise sayings attributed to Jesus, often called parables, are like miracle stories in being told to glorify the wisdom of Jesus, without having any real relevance to the issue Jesus faced. The authentic stories not only meet Dr. Grant's criteria (p. 90) but they are also relevant to the patriotic outcry which caused the crucifixion.

In discussing L, (above, p. 89), we noticed that even genuine parables are often given misleading interpretations. Stripped of these misinterpretations, all of them show the forceful way in which Jesus answered the criticisms which greeted his message.

Against the insistence that the Kingdom had already been promised to the Jews, Jesus told the story of the marriage feast given to outsiders because the invited guests had excused themselves (Lk 14.15-24).

To the protest that further concessions to the Romans would bring starvation to the Jews, Jesus told of widows and neighbors who were helped when in need (Lk 11.5-8; 18.1-6). To those who had tried kindness, but claimed that the Romans understood only force, Jesus told the story of the sower (Lk 4.1-20): much of your seed may be wasted, but there is no other way to produce crops than to sow seed.

The Didache

The Didache is our third and final document (along with "L" and the Logia [Q]) which fulfills Professor Grant's criteria for an early work.

The Didache gives us no new information about Jesus, but since it is a modified form of Q (Messianistic rituals to which some teachings of Jesus have been added) it gives us a glimpse into the history of the formation of the Gospels. By studying the changes we get a better idea of how the Gospels developed. (The Didache, with differing scholarly opinions on it, is available in C. C. Richardson's "Early Christian Fathers," Westminster, 1970, pp. 161-179).

The Didache must have served the same purpose as Q, for it also is a manual of disciplines to which some teachings of Jesus have been added. Traditionalists suppose that these teachings were taken from the canonical Gospel of Matthew; therefore they contend that this manual is later than AD 90.

On the other hand, naturalists observe (a) that the rituals for baptism and the eucharistic blessing in the Didache come from the Essenes, not the Gospels; (b) that the piety and emphasis on ritualistic forms is similar to the disciplines of the Dead Sea Scrolls; (c) that the Didache breaks with the teachings of John the Baptist, has not heard of Paul, and has only scant knowledge of the teachings of Jesus, (d) the Didache does not summarize the whole gospel, but only its most primitive "oral" core.

There are many later "Christianizing" additions to the Didache. Its title, "Teachings of the Twelve Apostles," must be later than Mark's creation of chosen "disciples" (AD 65). The trinitarian formula for baptism (Did 7.1-4) must come from the second century or later. On the other hand, uncertainties as to baptismal water (Did 7.2) show that the rules were not yet fully established. The Lord's Prayer (Did 8.2) is another Messianistic contribution. The fact that the Didache does not do Jesus the honor of mentioning him, indicates a period before Jesus was thought of as an authority.

Barnabus could have taken the Didache with him when he went to teach "the first Christians" in Antioch (ca AD 40). Presumably, if he had known anything of the miracle stories, or of the Resurrection myth, these reports would have appeared in the Didache. The document has carried authority such as only the original Jerusalem church could have given it.

Chapter 7. THE MYTHOLOGICAL TEXTS

Earlier chapters have given my reasons for accepting the naturalistic portions of the Gospels; I must now summarize my reasons for rejecting the portions which present Jesus as a supernatural Christ.

The Gospel of Mark

Since Mark's document was the earliest of the four New Testament Gospels to be completed, it was formerly supposed that it was the most accurate. Furthermore, since Mark says nothing about loving the enemy, but does have an extended chapter (Mk 13) on the end of the world, supernaturalists have argued that "eschatology," a prophecy of the end, was Jesus' central theme.

Although Mark's account is most graphic, it

is the primary source for the supernatural picture
of Jesus. Nearly two-thirds of the miracle stories come to us through Mark, but he gives nothing
of Jesus' sermons, and only a few misconstrued
parables. Mark's main effort is directed toward
combatting the naturalism of the Logia, which was
written a few years earlier.

Scholars are beginning to speak out against
these misrepresentations. Father Nolan, a Provincial Superior of the Dominican Order, says:

> Jesus has been more frequently hon-
> ored and worshipped for what he did
> not mean than for what he did mean.
> The supreme irony is that some of the
> things he opposed most strongly...
> were resurrected, preached and
> spread... in his name. Jesus cannot
> be fully identified with the great
> religious phenomenon ... known as
> Christianity. -- Albert Nolan,
> "Jesus Before Christianity," Orbis,
> Maryknoll, 1978, p. 3.

Mark's Gospel is perhaps most responsible for
this irony. The deaths of Peter and Paul (in about
AD 64) had left the church with no one who claimed
first-hand knowledge of a supernatural Jesus.
Besides, the failure of Jesus to return at once as
expected was devastating to the new faith.

Mark had to do his best to revive the supernatural hope, otherwise the Christian church would collapse, as indeed it did in Palestine where Mark's Gospel was rejected.

It is not reported that Mark made any speeches, but his skill in writing is evident. His Gospel displays a remarkable gift for inventing interesting settings and realistic conversations for his stories. Few writers have succeeded as well as he in making the incredible seem believable.

Yet, to suit his purpose, he garbled the report of the temptations of Jesus, he distorted the parable of the Sower, he created the myth of secrecy as an explanation for the general ignorance about Jesus, and he condemned as faithless the relatives and neighbors to whom we are most indebted for our knowledge of the natural Jesus.

It seems significant that the authors of Matthew's and of Luke's Gospels could find nothing to support Mark's stories except Mark's Gospel, and they copied most of it word for word. Besides, the formula for Q recognizes that anything in Mark is less authentic than Matthew or Luke.

The Gospel of Matthew

The Gospel of Matthew was compiled by a Jewish Christian around AD 80 to make the Jesus of

Paul and Mark more acceptable in Palestine.

The Jews had rejected Mark's Gospel because it supported Paul's claim that Jesus had the supernatural power to set aside the Jewish law and grant salvation on the basis of faith in Christ.

The compiler of Matthew could hardly wait through the introduction to the Sermon on the Mount before insisting that Jesus was in full support of the Mosaic Law (Matt. 5.17-19). Actually, we don't know what position Jesus would have taken, since Paul did not raise this question until long after the Crucifixion.

Of the new items which Matthew presents, Professor Emil Kraeling says:

> These materials... are of value to the historian chiefly as testimonies... of the faith and life of the author and of the Christian group he represented... [They] hardly add to dependable knowledge. -- E. G. Kraeling, "The Clarified New Testament: The Four Gospels," by permission from McGraw-Hill, 1962, p. 115.

The Gospel of Luke

Luke's Gospel seems to have been written after Matthew was compiled. However, since Luke traveled widely with Paul from about AD 50, he began his investigations earlier, they lasted longer, and covered more places than did those of the compiler of Matthew.

As a professional researcher Luke would have been eager to add confirming details to Mark's stories, but he finds only the L source. In his search for all authentic details (Lk 1.3ff), Luke must have been eager to go to Galilee where Jesus had done most of his preaching, but he could find no one there who knew anything about a supernatural Jesus.

Luke stayed two years with Philip in Caesarea (Acts 21.8, 10; 24.27). Philip was one of the first to spread the word about Jesus, but even he knew nothing about a miraculous Jesus or "twelve apostles." As a result, Luke thought that Mark's "Apostle Philip" must have been someone else. The only reported sermon of the Philip whom Luke visited was from Isaiah, rather than from John the Baptist, another indication of authenticity.

Surely Luke could have found others who had known Jesus if he had been willing to accept naturalistic reports. Luke's confusion over Philip's status is evidence, not only of the lack of other first-hand reports, but also of the lack of twelve authoritative sources. In Luke's eye-witness section of Acts, Philip is the only first-hand contact mentioned who could have been a source of independent information.

The Gospel of John

Studies have led many scholars to believe that John's Gospel is not by "the beloved disciple," as had been supposed. The picture in John is so contrary to that of the earlier Gospels that one or the other must be misleading. For example, the earlier reports have Jesus say, "Why do you call me good? No one is good but God" (Lk 18.19), but in John, Jesus says, "I and my father are one" (Jn 10.30).

Again, in John's story of the raising of Lazarus (Jn 11), a crowd witnesses this public demonstration so that all will know that Jesus has power over death. Yet, in the earlier Gospels no one knows this amazing story, not even Luke who made a "diligent study of all things known about Jesus" (Lk 1.1-4).

It is generally agreed that the John who wrote this Gospel was the Elder John, of Ephesus, a popular mystic who wrote the epistles of John at the beginning of the second century.

He does not claim to have actually seen Jesus, nor to have been a member of any authorized group of twelve disciples, but he claims to have had a vision. John's authority, like Paul's, depended on an apparition of Jesus. Yet these visionary views were responsible for changing Jesus from a natural into a supernatural figure.

This has handicapped the development of a spiritually mature religion.

John's Gospel makes use of the metaphors which Paul and others had used, to create a supernatural Christ. Jesus as "the wine of life," developed into the story of the water made into wine (Jn 2.1-11); Jesus as the "water of life" grew into the story of the woman at the well who needed water (Jn 4.1-30); the metaphor of Jesus the life-giver was changed into the story of the resurrection of Lazarus (Jn 11.1-46).

John's Gospel is prized for its call (Jn 14) to mystical unity between God and man. Mysticism as the concern to bring unity between god (the potential for spiritual maturity) and man (the human will to fulfill that potential) is as important to naturalism as it was to John.

However, John's mysticism was limited by arbitrary ideas about God and the goal. It offers heavenly mansions as the reward for unity (Jn 14.2) rather than the satisfaction of becoming a mature human being. Nothing does more to prevent a person from fulfilling his potentials than the childish hope that a supernatural spirit will bring all one wants as a reward for the right faith. Civilization flounders because religion has encouraged false hopes, rather than maturity.

In naturalism, the source is not separated from humanity. The feeling of separation has been caused by allowing brute survival needs to separate us from our distinctive humanity. If we are to become our true selves, we have to separate ourselves from the brute but not from our humanity. John's Gospel offers little help toward true mysticism, and no help in recovering the historical Jesus.

The Resurrection Stories

Like the nativity legends, the resurrection reports are separate myths. Harry Emerson Fosdick suggested that instead of an empty tomb leading to doctrines of immortality, "the development may have been in precisely the opposite direction."

Certainly if the idea of Jesus' risen life started from any factual element associated with an empty tomb, that element was never clearly visualized, even in the imagination of the first disciples, and is now confused for us in narratives that contradict each other in every important detail. -- H. E. Fosdick, "Guide to Understanding the Bible," Harper, 1938, pp. 292-294.

Walter Bundy voices similar doubts:
Out of the ressurection tradition the historian sifts a single historical

> fact, not the resurrection of Jesus,
> but the early Christian belief in
> that resurrection... This faith is
> older than the resurrection tradi-
> tion, in fact the stories are the
> product of that faith, not its found-
> ation. -- Walter Bundy, "Jesus and
> the First Three Gospels," Harvard,
> 1955, p. 555.

Although Mark's Gospel originally said nothing about a resurrection, defenders of the doctrine point out that Paul had taught it fifteen
years earlier. But that suggests that Mark must
have known the resurrection stories but rejected
them, perhaps in favor of Stephen's view. Paul's
doctrine was based not on a belief in an empty
tomb, but on visions of Jesus. Apparitions of
murdered men were common, and it is clear that the
church was not impressed by them at first.

Several scholars, including the Abbé Loisy
and A. P. Davies, are convinced that it was
Stephen's vision of Jesus in heaven which first
excited belief that Jesus was still alive (Acts
7.55).

Stephen's vision was impressive because it
came just before his own martyrdom; it was not a
vision of Jesus resurrected on earth, but in heav-
en. There is no evidence that anyone was believ-

ing that Jesus was resurrected until Stephen had his vision.

Stephen's apparition had a revolutionary effect; it led the Jerusalem Messianists to believe that the obscure Jesus was the man for whom they had been looking, and that he was ready to return to earth to complete his Messianic mission which had been cut short.

The Apostle Paul

Since we have Paul's Epistles, practically unchanged from the 40s and 50s of the first century, well before our earliest Gospel, Mark (ca 65), some scholars have considered Paul our best authority on Jesus.

Furthermore, it was not the teachings of Jesus but of Paul that first attracted a following: it was Paul's hope of supernatural salvation which produced the Christian church. The Gospels were written to support Paul's doctrines, not to present a historical account of Jesus. The Gospel writers thought that Jesus was supernatural because they had the writings of Paul, not because they had first-hand evidence.

As previously stated, Paul had been raised as a pious Hebrew in Asia Minor where his boyhood associates were not Jews but pagans. Paul wanted to convert his friends to the worship of the one true God. Therefore, instead of the common Jewish hope of destroying the Romans and saving the Jews, Paul wanted to save the Romans and destroy the fanatical messianistic Jews whose hostility to the Empire was making it more difficult to convert the pagans to the worship of Jehovah. When Paul went to Jerusalem to study theology, he joined others in harassing the Messianists.

In the midst of Paul's persecution of the Messianists, he had a sudden change of heart (Acts 26.12-16). It is possible that he had heard that Jesus had urged love for the Romans; surely he had been informed that the Messianists were converting pagans. Paul lamented his own inability to win Gentiles because of their opposition to the arbitrary Jewish religious requirements.

The success of the Messianists of Antioch in attracting pagans led Paul to the sudden conviction that, if Jesus were indeed God's chosen Messiah, his suffering on the cross would provide the blood redemption which had appealed so strongly to the pagans in Mithraism. Jesus' blood would recompense God for setting aside the law of circumcision. Few people today think they must appease God for not being circumcised, but to Paul this idea was the inspiration that made him a Christian.

In many ways Paul was a mature spiritual

leader, but the immaturity of some of his ideas is evident:

> The Lord himself shall descend from
> heaven with a shout, and with the
> sound of trumpets, and the dead in
> Christ shall rise first; then we
> which are alive shall be caught up
> together with them in the clouds to
> meet the Lord in the air (I Thes.
> 4.16ff).

Paul boasts that his ideas about Jesus did not come from any flesh and blood person; they were his own inspiration (Gal. 1.12, 16, 17; 2.6). Paul's promise of salvation from death and circumcision through faith in his supernatural Christ attracted fanatical devotion, but it is doubtful whether it attracted much spiritual maturity.

In theory Paul put love above doctrine, but in practice, Paul's supernaturalism encouraged hostility to differences of belief. Like all supernaturalism it was an arbitrary faith, not only attracting people with glowing promises, but threatening them with dire consequences if they did not conform.

Since Paul's myths have converted much of the world, it is often argued that they should be retained even though Paul did invent them.

Unfortunately, his myths have also encouraged false hopes rather than personal responsibility;

they have led nations to boast of divine favors, rather than to search for better understanding; they have fostered sectarian divisions; they have encouraged rituals for worship rather than training in spiritual expression; and they have kept civilization from cultivating the maturity needed for human survival.

The oral tradition

Since there was no written Gospel for the first twenty years after the Crucifixion, many people have supposed that the early Christians memorized the words of Jesus, and told his story orally. To be sure, after he was accepted by the Messianists as the man for whom they had been looking, rumors of his miracles were popular, and they grew with the retelling. But there is little evidence of an oral tradition for the Logia, or of the historical Jesus.

If a savior on whom the salvation of the world depended had twelve reliable disciples, they could have seen to it that their precious knowledge was carefully reported. Unfortunately, scholars have had to conclude that the "chosen twelve" are part of the myth.

Here everything is an open question.
Their identity is a later idea...
About their activity hardly anything

tangible is told. Except for Peter,
they disappear from history without
leaving a trace. -- Hans Conzelman,
"History of Primitive Christianity,"
Abingdon, 1972, p. 54 ff.

We have been seeking the authentic in the
Gospels, not that we might have authoritative
instructions from Jesus, but that we might have a
clearer understanding of the problem we face in
turning our traditional religion from its authoritarian claims.

Criteria of Authenticity

On page 90 I noted five criteria of authenticity which Professor Grant developed from his
studies. I now add four from my own observations:

(a) The clarity of Jesus. The Gospels often
attribute trivial and contradictory statements to
Jesus. The authentic portions give no suggestion
that Jesus shared John the Baptist's false hope of
destroying the Roman Empire with fire from heaven.
Where the Gospels create the impression that Jesus
had lost touch with reality, it is now apparent
that the Gospels had lost touch with Jesus.

(b) Simplicity. The humility and obscurity
of the authentic Jesus is in sharp contrast to the
magnificence attributed to him by those who never
knew him; the Epistle of James, the Didache, and

the Logia show no deference to Jesus. R. B.
Lightfoot of Oxford observed that even the myths
have to explain why "people failed to understand,
reverence, and accept him," and why "his life on
earth had passed unrecognized and unacclaimed."
-- R. B. Lightfoot, "History and Interpretation in
the Gospels," Hodder & Stoughton (pp. 74, 82,
102).

(c) Impartiality. Jesus' chief reason for
rejecting John's hope was his observation that
god, like nature, is impartial.

(d) No doubt Jesus tried to help the sick,
but those who knew Jesus had no reason to make his
help seem supernatural or exorcistic.

Conclusion

Jesus told the story of a traveler walking to
Jericho who was robbed and left half-dead by the
roadside. A passing enemy stopped and did all he
could to help the injured man. Perhaps real enemies never act that way, but Jesus did not ask
whether the act of generosity was common; he asked
if it was neighborly. Today our streets are still
unsafe, democracy is in danger.

When schools thought that education was a
matter of teaching certain beliefs, learning decayed. At present spirituality is decaying because our religious institutions suppose that

their business is to get people to accept a supernatural God. In Jesus' day the problem was the
survival of the Jewish nation; at present we are
faced with a threat to humanity. The solution is
not to maintain the arbitrary beliefs of the past,
but to give attention to fulfilling the human
potential for spiritual growth and maturity.

PART III

THE MATURE SPIRIT IN PRACTICE

PART III

THE MATURE SPIRIT IN PRACTICE

Chapter 8. THE LOVING SPIRIT

The final section of this book deals with the practical implications of the mature spirit. Readers who regard religion as having to do primarily with sacred or biblical concerns, may have difficulty reconciling these practical matters with their concept of religion as an enterprise devoted to a worship of the holy, or heavenly.

We cannot proceed without giving attention to this major difference in religious outlooks. People have been taught such reverence for the source of life that they are often shocked by the very thought of being a partner in the creative process rather than a worshipper of the creator.

We realize that human intelligence was required to invent language. The same use of intelligence is necessary for the development of the
mature spirit. The world is not guaranteed to
succeed. We have to seek the solutions to our
problems.

The idea that the world was created by an
all-powerful authority was responsible for developing the concept of a God so holy, so able to get
along without human help that human duties could
be satisfied by singing God's praises. A more
realistic view of the creative process recalls us
to a more practical religion.

The neo-orthodox concept of an aloof, sacred
God has won such a hold upon theological thinking
in the present century that one now has only to
call a clergyman "secular" or a preacher of the
"social Gospel" and he or she is excluded from
religious consideration. This attitude tends to
restrict spirituality to sacrosanct concerns. To
the contrary, I view spirituality as the most
mature and practical aspect of life.

In the pre-evolutionary view, the whole creative process was thought to be the expression of
an arbitrary authority who willfully determined
what should or should not be. We still find deter-
mining factors in events, but we now see them as
growing out of physical requirements, rather than
out of arbitrary commands.

This new view of the universe demands a new concept of the creative spirit, or first cause. Instead of being content with an authoritarian spirituality, we now need to cultivate the mature spirit. Instead of obeying the arbitrary commands of scripture we now have to use our intelligence to discover our spiritual duties and responsibilities.

The hope of authoritarian direction makes people more stubborn and arbitrary, rather than more willing to find spiritual solutions to problems. We have military plans for destroying the world, but no rational program for cultivating the spirit needed to save the world.

The ancient hope that a Messiah would be sent to save the world is no longer regarded as realistic by people who understand the present world situation. Our hopes may still be high, but they are hopes in the transforming power of the mature human spirit, rather than in heavenly angels.

The Religion of Lovingkindness

It may seem sweet to feel the presence of a God who personally cares for us and makes everything work out for the best. But nothing does more to discourage the development of the spirit which actually does make things work better, than the belief that the work of our salvation has already been done for us. The ancient religious belief in magic formulas for salvation made people more willing to risk war or death, but less willing to actually develop the loving, considerate spirit needed to solve our problems.

It was for this reason that the poet Sarah Cleghorn suggested substituting the name "Lovingkindness" for "God."

> There is one simple device for realizing how clear... is the religion of lovingkindness. This is to substitute... the word "love" (or lovingkindness) for the word "God"... No sooner does one use the realistic name for the divine element in life than the [first] Commandment appears to be the very embodiment of the natural goodness of the human heart. 'Thou shalt have no other gods than Lovingkindness.' The clarifying effect of introducing the supreme authority of Lovingkindness into our daily difficulties... goes further than calming worry and distraction... The simplicity of trying to serve or demonstrate Lovingkindness releases our natural intuition of where to go, what to say or write... How Lovingkindness springs up in the heart! To

our great wonder, we hear it sounding
sweet in our own voices, feel it
looking out of our dim and reddened
eyes and giving our shaking hands a
thrilling tender touch. -- Sarah
Cleghorn, "The Seamless Robe," Macmillan, 1945, pp. 14-16.

Sarah Cleghorn saw "prayer" as "communion
between man's will to bless and its immortal
spring." This communion came without effort when
one abandoned false images and began to develop a
spirit of lovingkindness.

I have known Methodists who claimed a "second
blessing," Quakers who have heard divine voices,
Catholics who would gladly die for their faith, or
neo-orthodox ministers who made their Christianity
a persistent irritant in their relationship with
other people. They seemed to think that their
piety was more important than the spirit of lovingkindness.

Sarah Cleghorn would no more have mentioned
her religious preference than she would have
boasted about her college. When you are practicing lovingkindness, your credentials are not important. If we are to be opposed, let it be for
practicing a magnanimous spirit, not for being
contentious about our beliefs.

Creating social harmony

Mature spirituality is marked primarily by loving, social concerns. This was as true of colonial deism, and of modernism, as it is now. Reactionary religion, like reactionary politics, shows itself by a lack of social concern. Materialism is a turning away from human need.

Fortunately there are signs of a spiritual awakening. The failure of orthodoxy to meet our present spiritual need is obvious. The religion of lovingkindness, a religion for the cultivation of the mature spirit, is being demanded. What we need is the clear articulation of that spirit, an articulation which you and I need to be giving it.

The people of Spain, in their civil war of 1936-9, could hardly be blamed for not knowing which side to choose. Their religious institutions were on the side of the fascists; sound economics, national self-interest, even the popular will seemed to support fascism. How was the ordinary person to know that fascism was really on the side of a brute insensitivity which human society could not and would not tolerate?

The vital question was not, "Where does the church, the majority, sound economics, or national self-interest lie?" The real question was, "On which side is the human spirit, the spirit of maturity, of democracy?

Lovingkindness does not have any army divisions, but we cannot allow ourselves to be misled by popularity, tradition, or the arguments of imperialists. Instead we have to ask, "Which side has the better appreciation for the human, the democratic spirit? Humanity may still be immature, but it is learning that its survival depends upon rejecting the brute. We are desperate for the religion of lovingkindness.

Chapter 9. MORAL PROBLEMS

The Present Moral Uncertainty

The scientific temper of our age discourages
doctors, lawyers, or even the clergy, from being
critical of behavior. This professional attitude
has filtered down to all of us. Today most people
maintain loyalty and care for neighbors and
friends regardless of their conduct. Valuable as
this attitude of acceptance is, it creates the
impression that there are no longer any moral
standards.

Naturalism especially has been accused of
moral indifference. But although naturalism calls
all reality "natural," yet it does not regard
everything as good. Weeds are just as natural as
roses, but only those things are called "good"
which contribute toward one's goals or needs,

including the magnanimous spirit. A farmer keeps busy destroying the weeds and other foes of his garden. If we care about fulfilling our mature spiritual potentials we will be diligent in protecting and cultivating them.

Sometimes it is argued that any culture that has survived, or any behavior that does no physical harm, is normal and should not be criticized.

On the contrary, a mechanic, for example, is not content with an automobile that can only chug down the road but is not performing up to its potential. The statistical average may be of interest to secondhand dealers, but to most people a "normal" car is one that is operating at full capacity.

Similarly, a normal person is one whose conduct and attitude enables him or her to fulfill his or her significant potentials.

Any style of living which produces human inadequacies, such as ignorance, stagnation, quarreling, alienation, irresponsibility, broken homes, or unhappiness is failing to meet essential standards no matter how long that culture has survived, or how widely that style of behavior has been accepted. We cannot be satisfied with any conduct, any educational system, any religion, which hinders rather than contributes to the fulfilling of human potentials for maturity in body, mind, and spirit.

Although I am also concerned about material injustices, in this chapter I will focus on injuries to the human spirit.

Since spiritual maturity is essential to the survival of humanness, it is of concern to all of us. Professional counselors often find it useful to remove any sense of guilt which might make their clients feel isolated. In contrast, I am assuming a normal eagerness to achieve human maturity. People do not want to know what excuses can be found for their failures; they want to find the road to spiritual success.

The Gandhian Model

Western religions have traditionally taken Jesus as their model. Naturalists find that unacceptable because it generally implies a fixed standard, rather than one that is developing.

Furthermore, the compilers of the Gospels were Messianists who gave us their preconceived idea of the man they supposed was about to provide their miraculous liberation from Rome. Consequently, we have little dependable knowledge concerning Jesus.

To use the example of one whose spiritual development was exceptional, let us consider Mahatma Gandhi. He was far from perfect, but few people have had his success in cultivating "Soul

Force," the power of the human spirit. Furthermore, we have quite accurate information about his
life and methods.

No one is so talented as to be able to a-
chieve worthwhile goals without accepting the
criticisms, the coaching, the rules needed for
attainment. Gandhi wrote a book of disciplines
for those who wanted to grow in the power of the
spirit. Some of his rules dealt with local problems, such as untouchability, or cottage indus-
tries. However, four of his prescriptions merit
our attention.

(a) **Devotions.** Every morning and evening
Gandhi held a meeting with friends to sing Hindu
hymns. He called these meetings "Yajna" or "Devotions," but he was careful to avoid giving the
impression that he was keeping these observances
in the hope of gaining supernatural power or influence. Gandhi's Yajna was largely an effort to
share in the religious life of his people. His
own spirit was strengthened and guided by periods
of meditation. These quiet times were efforts to
purify himself of self-interest so that he might
have the power and joy of love.

(b) **Non-possession, or poverty.** Buddha, St.
Francis, and many other religious leaders have
insisted that the serious seeker for spirituality
had to become a beggar. Gandhi did not beg but he
did emphasize simplicity, so as to be unencum-

bered. He realized the necessity for material things and honored those who were good property managers. It could be argued against poverty that some possessions may help spiritual growth, while economic want has deprived more people of spiritual maturity than it has enriched. Yet many serious seekers have found that voluntary simplicity is required for spiritual fulfillment.

(c) **Control of the palate.** Gandhi did not use meat, tobacco, or alcohol. Were these restrictions necessary? Granted that some remarkably mature people have not observed them, while some others who have adopted them have failed to develop love and forebearance, yet no one can hope to have sufficient time and energy for spiritual development who does not subordinate his insistent physical desires.

(d) **Chastity.** Gandhi's personal rule of "celibacy," or total abstinence from sexual intercourse, weakened the force of his more general rule, "chastity," the disciplining of sexual impulses. He pointed out that "to hear suggestive stories, or to see suggestive sights," is destructive of the spiritual nourishment that comes through sex.

Gandhi's disciplines did not encourage a type of spirituality which is satisfied with inner peace and assurances of heavenly care. On the contrary they were directed toward his own need to grow in love and consideration for others.

Marriage and the Home

Changes in society may necessitate changes in moral requirements. A hundred years ago schooling was commonly finished at fifteen and marriage soon followed. Now the period for meeting academic demands is often twice as long. Since young people are usually not ready for the responsibilities of a home until they leave school and go to work, marriage must be delayed.

Consequently the moral problem has changed from one of enforcing celibacy among young people, to one of providing further understanding of, and appreciation for, the spiritual values of sex during this extended period of preparation. Arbitrary restrictions often vulgarize, or impede, spiritual growth.

Birth control provides a bridge across the pitfalls occasioned by the modern necessity for postponing marriage. The best guide is to consider what behavior is most likely to prepare for a happy and spiritually strong home.

In 1927 Judge Ben Lindsey of the Denver Juvenile Court began to call for temporary, or "companionate marriages" for the young who were not yet ready for life commitments. His efforts produced an almost unanimous protest from parents and teachers.

Today, we would be happy to get back to companionate marriages, since our moral situation has grown much worse. We now have almost totally unregulated and ill-considered relationships, creating an epidemic of promiscuity, disease, teen-age pregnancies, and meaningless sex, often producing the total destruction of the human spirit of caring and love.

Companionate marriages had the advantage of providing a basis for agreement and spiritual growth. The present lawless state of relationships has often reduced sex to mere "fun," when it could be our greatest force for spiritual maturity.

Commitment. Since protection against pregnancy has made sexual intimacy common among friends before marriage, it might be supposed that there is nothing wrong with it after but outside of marriage. However, marriage brings a commitment to making one's spouse and home happy and secure.

If one's spouse doesn't care, if he or she has no jealousy or interest in the stability and mutual responsibilities of the home, then we do not have a family which matters, or which stimulates spiritual growth. Just as the life that is unexamined is not worth living, so the uncommitted or unloved family is not worth having. The loss of one's spouse is a staggering blow to anyone with sensitivity. Unfaithfulness to one's spouse is a cruelty which no mature person would inflict.

Sex roles. When most people lived on farms, husbands usually ploughed the fields and cleaned the stables, while wives cooked the food and washed the clothes. The family was important and each member was eager to do whatever he or she could do best for it.

Today, home is sometimes thought to be a secondary or temporary interest. Yet most of life's joys and sorrows, its happinesses and tragedies, its spiritual success or failure, come from the home. If homes were only a place for sexual satisfaction, it would be secondary; men and women could encourage one another to be independent so that sex might be enjoyed without obligation. But the satisfactions of maturity come from accepting the responsibilities of home, not from escaping them.

Children need both a father and a mother. Homes are not built by offering freedom from the responsibilities of these roles; they are built by men and women who are willing to sacrifice for their families and who find a satisfying place for each member. Nothing is more likely to ruin a man or a woman than for someone to take over his or her duties completely. Responsibility is a necessity for maturity; it must be recognized, respected, and developed.

Some people think of physical harm as the only evil, and condone any sexual deviation so long as it is physically harmless. Deviations may seem exciting or attractive, but they are often detrimental to the responsibilities of family life and to the discipline needed to coach the spirit in love, responsibility, and patience.

Control of population. Generally when population is reduced, competition slackens, and the needs of families for longer and greater care have a chance to expand. Spirituality has evolved, usually, where the survival competition was not too pressing.

If now world population is to rise to the maximum number that can be fed, it is probable that the physical struggle for food will again dominate, and the human race will revert to the brute. Since morality is a matter of protecting the spiritual life, population control is one of our greatest moral necessities.

Abortion. A fetus may have the potential for becoming a mature human spirit, but to treat a potential as though it were a fulfillment destroys the capacity to deal intelligently with human developments. Maturity demands consideration for all factors, not an arbitrary insistence on one. Albert Schweitzer's "reverence for life" did not mean avoiding destruction, but avoiding hostility, scorn, or indifference. We have to consider the spiritual harm caused by over-population, and by unwanted births.

Since children have a right to be born healthy, and with loving parents, how can society insist that every living fetus be brought to birth? On the contrary, we have an obligation to protect the right of every baby to be well-born.

We need to develop our own responsibilities in today's world. Ancient religions are immoral in offering the comforts and promises which are attractive, rather than the challenges and sensitivity needed for maturity. Modern society is destroying itself for want of adequate spiritual understanding and cultivation. We should be developing religious institutions which recognize and strive to fulfill the requirements for full humanness.

Chapter 10. CIVIC IMPLICATIONS

The mature spirit is the democratic spirit.
It is no accident that "civic" and "civil" come
from the same root. To be civil is to be polite,
fair-minded, considerate of others. It may be
impossible to "love our enemies" in the way we
love our families, but in civic affairs it is
possible, and even necessary, to be civil and
fair-minded toward our opponents.

The democratic spirit has been found so helpful in democratic debate that it is now used in
all forms of discussion. No one strengthens his
argument by making a personal attack on his opponent; the more respect one shows for his opposition, the more force do his arguments have. This
attitude of fair-minded respect and consideration
is what we mean by "the democratic spirit." It is

the application of the spirit of lovingkindness to civic activities.

When it was supposed that spirituality had to do with an entirely different, a non-secular world, it was thought that authoritarianism could be maintained in religion, even though one demanded democratic consideration for opponents in secular matters. However, those who accept the reality of one world find it necessary to be fairminded and considerate in religion also. The democratic spirit eliminates authoritarianism in spiritual as well as in civic affairs.

A few years ago both the United States and Russia agreed that nuclear war was intolerable. Neither side could claim authority over the other side. This has made it necessary to co-exist, to apply the spirit of respect and consideration to our opponents in international matters. We have to settle all differences, religious as well as civic, in the spirit of democracy, rather than in an authoritarian manner.

The United States helped set up the World Court as an independent body of judicial opinion to which disputes could be referred. Is it not authoritarian to decide that our national interests take precedence over the rule of law, as the United States did in the 1980's?

Surely in the long run it is not in our interest to take that anti-democratic position.

To co-exist we must get rid of the authoritarian and the anti-democratic spirit.

In discussing the Gospels (above, pp 69ff) I called attention to Jesus' opposition to the popular but unrealistic hope for an arbitrary or authoritarian liberation from Rome. In Jesus' view a reformed spirituality was the only salvation for his nation. Events proved Jesus correct in rejecting John's hope for a Messianic liberation.

Today, we may no longer hope that an army from heaven will come to our defense, but we still believe in military, instead of spiritual, power. We still dream of being able to decide the fate of the world by force. We are in danger of annihilating ourselves because we have not the wit to see what Jesus saw, that our only hope of salvation is in cultivating the spirit of respect and appreciation.

We have forgotten that our own evolutionary experience proved the human spirit to be mightier than brute strength. Our prehistoric ancestors, in their struggle to emerge from the brute, found the human spirit victorious.

Our American Revolution was won against superior physical power because of our spiritual advantage. The poverty-stricken Vietnamese won against our superior might simply because our force was not enough to subdue them.

When the nations of the world have agreed to settle their disputes without resort to violence, it has not been because they are utopian, but because they see that arbitrary authority can no longer prevail among human beings.

The German people seemed to be spiritually mature, yet they allowed Hitler's confidence in military might to lead them into their worst disaster.

Germany was neither the first nor the last to lose its way: France under Napoleon, even the United States in Vietnam, are other examples. The brute looks strong, but the human spirit is more powerful.

Democracy has no magical power; it too has often failed. It is like seed: in spite of crop failures, we have to plant what we want to grow, or we get only weeds.

As population increases, it is inevitable that governments will need to exercise greater control over society. We see this in such a simple matter as traffic: the more traffic, the more traffic controllers we need. The question is, will these controls be applied in the democratic spirit? We must have the religious or other institutions for cultivating this spirit, so that we may be able to avoid the disaster of fascism or other authoritarian solutions.

Our Spiritual Needs in Economic Matters

Economists recognize a principle known as "The Iron Law of Wages." The theory is that when land is free and population is limited, employers have to compete for workers, and wages go up. But when land is limited and workers plentiful, workers have to compete for jobs, and wages keep going down to a bare subsistence level, unless some other agency such as unions, or governments, are able to give wages the protection they need.

Here again we find that controls require the democratic spirit. Laws and unions are useless as means of protecting the workers unless we have the democratic spirit.

If our religious societies were performing their true function, cultivating the human spirit, the crisis could be met. But how can we hope to have democratic relations in labor or anything else when many of our institutions are cultivating selfishness? What kind of "religion" is being fed us if it does nothing to touch our most profound spiritual needs?

Another important problem which has received almost no attention in America is the need to protect the good. Economists have a rule which states that bad money drives out good. That is the reason for our strict laws against counterfeiters. It is easier to rob the public by imitating the good than by picking pockets.

Yet there are serious reformers who continue to oppose regulations, falsely assuming that the good can take care of itself.

For example, Milton asked, "Whoever saw Truth put to the worse in a free and open encounter?" But Lowell found that "Truth [is] forever on the scaffold, Wrong [is] forever on the throne."

Milton's statement is like asking, "Whoever saw flowers overgrown with weeds?" Of course Truth will be worsted if it is not staunchly defended and protected. The reason we have gardeners is because without them our gardens would be overcome with weeds. To think that truth and decency do not need protective laws is utopianism of the worst kind.

To Offer Dignity

The Aquino revolution of 1986 in the Philippines was an important development in democratic confrontations. It has not solved all the problems of those islands, but its initial victory was impressive.

Mrs. Aquino defined democracy as "alydangyl," which means "to offer dignity." That is a good definition of the mature spirit also, as it offers appreciation and respect, and is non-authoritarian.

Those who think only in terms of primitive force suppose that such concessions would result in being swallowed up, but those who recognize the power of the democratic spirit recognize that these concessions are necessary for growth. Granting dignity implies recognition of one's common humanity with others.

All too often, people through the ages have acted on the idea that beliefs are more important than our common humanity. But if a Christian, a Hindu, a Catholic, or a Moslem are all simply **human**, they already share the highest basis for mutual respect.

The United Nations. It is often supposed that the United Nations could be made more effective by giving it more power. But when Eleanor Roosevelt was the American delegate, she gave respect and dignity to everyone, and America did not need to claim superior rights or power. Eleanor Roosevelt's spirit gave the whole organization respect and dignity; America claimed no superior power, and the UN became an effective peace-keeping organization.

Since then America has often showed disrespect for others; as a result the organization has become weaker and America has become isolated.

The United Nations may not need a more perfect form, but it does need strong upholders of the democratic spirit. A show of brute strength may be more popular with us, but we must beware: it is surprising how rapidly fascism spread from Italy to Spain, Germany, and Japan as soon as cultivation of the democratic spirit was relaxed. We have to look beyond the glittering promises of physical force, to its final outcome.

Chapter 11. THE NEW REFORMATION

Recently a Jesuit chaplain at a state university told me that he too had given up the idea of God as a person, but he asked, "What are we to do? How are we to maintain an effective religious position without the myth of such a God?"

Anyone who has ever attempted even a modest change in religion will understand the perplexity of this chaplain at the prospect of attempting a major reform. Rarely does one find a single Baptist, Presbyterian, Moslem, Jew or Catholic who makes a significant change in his or her religion.

Those who have changed, more frequently have moved backward toward irresponsible hopes, rather than forward toward mature responsibilities. However, that may be because the issue was presented as a choice between heaven and hell, rather than as a choice between the limitations of infancy, and the significant opportunities of maturity.

What can any one person do to help build a mature religion for our society which needs one so much? The answer to the chaplain's question depends largely upon the individual's ability, situation, and opportunities.

We might change religions either by building new ones, or by reforming old ones.

In reform we could keep the old buildings, clergy, membership, and perhaps even the rituals, but change their meaning and purpose. Instead of insisting that the incarnation of the spiritual potential was a unique entrance of a personal God upon the stage of history, the church would recognize that the spirit must be manifested in every individual.

Instead of insisting on the divine accuracy of its beliefs, the church would cultivate the magnanimous spirit, such as was found in Gandhi, Schweitzer, and in compassionate, responsible people everywhere. Medieval universities, such as Oxford and Cambridge, were transformed into modern institutions by gradual reforms.

There may no longer be time for such a slow process; people often linger on the path of irresponsibility until it is too late. The fate of Jerusalem did not wait for the people to develop magnanimity. A more rapid change may be necessary if we are to escape nuclear annihilation.

If churches, mosques, and synagogues are unwilling to change fast enough, it may become necessary to create new religious institutions. Reform of the old would be better since there is a great store of moral and spiritual concern in the old institutions which is likely to suffer loss in a more radical change. But, for the survival of humanity, we must learn to cultivate the spirit as freely as we educate the mind.

Religious people often suppose that their doctrines were revealed by God and must not be tampered with. Their beliefs may cause wars, and do nothing to enrich the spirit, yet their adherents think it their duty to preserve them at all costs.

Some people complain that they are not spiritually fed by anything but their familiar rituals, but their spirituality is not the kind that needs to be cultivated for maturity.

Fellowship

No matter how discouraged one may be with his own religious community, one has to remember that spiritual growth depends upon learning patience, understanding, and appreciation for other points of view. For our own ripening we need to find, or

develop, a spiritually mature religious fellowship.

The members of one's professional or athletic
club may be more flexible and eager for spiritual
growth than are the people in one's church. Magnanimity is needed in all areas of society. A
club's donations to the poor are but a token of
the spirit to be cultivated.

Not only do we need fellowship, we also need
the courage to stand alone when necessary. Modernism failed, in part, because when Barth and
Niebuhr attacked, there was no determined resistance to this revival of authoritarian doctrines.
Roses may grow unaided, but so will the weeds; we
have to work.

Some Problems of Reform

When individuals or societies mature beyond
authoritarianism, they begin to show respect for
the opinions of others. This is what we mean by
"the democratic spirit."

It is often supposed that democracy means
"popular" government, or majority rule. To be
sure, "democracy" means government by the people,
but fascism was popularly supported. The rule of
childish or of mean-spirited people is not "democracy." Only in a nation of informed, fair-minded
people can we have a democracy.

Sooner or later, and either in an old institution or in a new one, a specific program for encouraging spiritual maturity will have to be developed.

How are we to imbue our group with a common purpose, without molding each into the same shape? Some in any group may be taking an interest in religion for the first time; others may be experienced theologians. Some may be eager to understand and develop the full implications of democratic, humanistic spirituality; others may have had their thinking halted somewhere, perhaps with Spinoza, Tom Paine, Emerson, or Fosdick. If there are those who have advanced only to a new level of authoritarianism, how is growth to be revived? How is each to be helped toward fulfilling his or her own spiritual potential?

It is understandable that worship should have been thought central to religion when it was supposed that God was a person who had willfully created the world, and who would reward in heaven those who honored him. But with a better understanding of the creative process, the presuppositions of the past will no longer do. Although the spirit of thankfulness is of value, our major concern is to fulfill the human potential, not simply to appreciate it.

No organism can be indifferent to its needs and goals. Hospitals cannot be flippant about physical care; teachers cannot be indifferent to learning; and no religious group will be respected if it is unconcerned about moral and spiritual growth. We have to be as careful as surgeons in maintaining our standards. The spirit is intangible, but therefore we need to be all the more clear and careful with it.

We may be able to learn from two examples of spiritual cultivation, one ancient, the other very recent.

The ancient Romans had the wit to see that the hearths around which their families gathered in times of danger, as well as in times of joy and fellowship, had been significant sources of their spiritual strength. Consequently they set up definite times each day for honoring the spirit of their homes.

This was in contrast to honoring tribal gods, as was done by many other people. In fact, the Romans did not propose to worship but simply to honor the spirit of their homes. They did not shut out those who disagreed with them, but they were firm in shutting out those who would defile or cheapen the spirit of their homes.

Unfortunately the Romans did not fully understand their ceremonies. Instead of honoring the domestic spirit of caring and responsibility, they began to make separate mental images of the spirit of their hearths, and to hope that an independent spirit of the home would give them health and prosperity if they used the right ritual.

Of course they found what seemed to be clear evidence that the rituals worked magic. Thus the honoring of the caring spirit was weakened. However, the Romans may have had the seeds of a more realistic religion for cultivating the mature spirit than we have derived from our Gospels.

The more recent example is taken from my home town. Our little village has a small, excellent college which for many years held daily Quaker services in a gothic-style hall. By 1970 these daily meetings had become futile; many of the students and faculty no longer believed in the type of spirituality represented by such exercises. Consequently the meetings were discontinued and the building fell into disuse.

In 1984 the college decided that the hall was too fine to remain idle. A committee was given two million dollars to remodel the structure, and in 1986 the building was reopened. The top level may now be used for dancing, receptions, and the like. The bottom floor might now be thought of as a Greek or Roman market, where people browse for books and other items for sale.

A middle floor is divided into many half-open, table-centered enclosures where spontaneous groups of students can gather for what used to be called "bull sessions." If a student is not interested in the topic under discussion in one group center, he or she can wander off to another partial enclosure which may be more congenial.

Some people lament the passing of the old hall for "Quaker meetings." They regard the change as a further "secularization" of the school.

Indeed the change is a "secularization" in the literal sense of being a turning to this world instead of toward a heavenly one, but not in the implied sense of being a turning away from spirituality. Actually the hall is now more spiritual in a democratic sense. It does not divide the students along creedal lines; mutual caring and concern are enhanced.

Recently twelve leading composers held a symposium at the college on contemporary music. The main concern of the participants was the wide gap between the popularity of "rock" music which provides noise and excitement but little esthetic content, as compared with the wide-spread neglect of classical music with its rich spiritual meanings.

The complaint of the musicians was similar to that which religious and even political leaders have been making since ancient times: the populace honors immaturity, leaving spiritually mature people to stand alone. Crowds went to hear John the Baptist promise help from heaven, while Jesus,

who called for love and reconciliation, was despised and rejected. Many people still suppose
that religious or democratic superiority is indi-
cated by the popular response elicited, rather
than by growth in the democratic spirit.

The Peril Facing Society

Most Jews in Jesus' day could see only the
peril posed by pagan Rome. Most people in America
today see only the threat of godless communism.
Jesus was not being sentimentally religious when
he declared that the real danger for the Jews lay
in their failure to develop an appreciation for
their enemies. Today we can see that Jesus was
right, and that we are facing the same peril
in our modern times.

Evidences of spiritual poverty in our pros-
perous economy are everywhere -- in communities
that are more interested in sports than in democracy, and in the attitude of "I'm not in business for my health," which is taken as an excuse
for barbaric behavior.

By borrowing two hundred billion dollars from
the future, a President is able to promise an
immediate reduction of $1800 in personal income
taxes. Since many people's vote can be bought for
$1800, our grandchildren will have to pay the
bill, with interest.

Meanwhile, our religious institutions claim tax exemption for telling people to hope for supernatural solutions to their problems!

If we would test religious worth by spiritual growth, we would see how woefully inadequate our religions have been.

Just as weeds resume growth as soon as weeding is stopped, so people return to primitive behavior as soon as spiritual cultivation is neglected. In choosing not to weed, we choose to let the weeds take control.

It took only twenty years for Germany to retreat from leadership in education, culture, and the humanities, to a position where intellect and democracy were ridiculed.

It was only forty years after Jesus' plea for reconciliation with Rome was snuffed out that the Jewish nation was destroyed.

It took nineteen hundred years to restore Israel; it may take much longer than that to restore civilization if atomic war should ever engulf us. Is our present religion equal to the task of averting disaster?

The situation is discouraging, with nations spending trillions on armaments while our institutions for cultivating the human spirit are absorbed in winning converts to their ancient creeds.

Reasons for Hope

Fortunately, there are people in all countries and in all religions who do believe in the mature spirit -- but democracy depends on having all people educated and spiritually developed. To permit large numbers of people to remain illiterate or spiritually insensitive is equivalent to allowing criminals or Hitler youth to control our streets.

Normal people have the potential and drive for human maturity. We would not need to worry about the possible triumph of the brute if our religions were faithfully cultivating the spirit of love and humanhood. We are in jeopardy because so many religious leaders have been putting their creeds and their authoritarian piety ahead of spiritual growth.

Since religions have generally defaulted on their spiritual responsibility, psychologists have tried to fill the gap. One of them, Harry Overstreet, in his book "The Mature Mind," has a chapter on "Religious Maturity" in which he says:

> Christian religion as we have known it... encourages... the individual to remain a dependent child... What we had from Jesus of Nazareth was an invitation to maturity... [His] insight so flatly contradicted the

going conceptions of that day that
those who were bred in those conceptions angrily crucified him... Here
was a mature man's declaration that
the way for a human being to save
himself is that of growing into the
fullness of his powers -- and into
the knowledge that the greatest of
these powers is love... We can live
happily with any religion that grand-
ly and staunchly holds to that belief... We cannot live happily with
any other.   -- H. A. Overstreet,
"The Mature Mind," W. W. Norton,
1949, pp. 263-272.

A Modern Samaritan

At one period during the Second World War, my
friend Charles Wellman was picketing the White
House day and night to protest the cruelty of
bombing civilian targets.

One night about 3 a.m., a poorly dressed man
staggering across Pennsylvania Avenue was hit by a
passing automobile and knocked unconscious against
the curb.

Although the streets seemed deserted, a small
group of spectators gathered around the fallen
man. A passing chauffered limousine slowed to a

stop and the passenger got out to inquire what had
happened. When he was told, the stranger saw to
it that the guards at the White House gate called
an ambulance. Then he was driven on.

The spectators were abuzz with curiosity.
Who was the stranger who had stopped at that late
hour to see that the man by the side of the road
was cared for?

Someone in the crowd identified him: he was
Justice Frank Murphy. His name was well-known at
the time, as the ex-governor of Michigan who had
failed re-election because of his sympathy for
some striking automobile workers. President
Franklin Roosevelt had recently appointed him to
the Supreme Court.

Somewhere Justice Murphy had learned that
neighborliness is a first test of the kind of
human beings we are supposed to be. There is no
magic in it. Neighborliness is not guaranteed to
succeed. But for how long has the human species
been trying to realize its spiritual potential?

In my view the purpose of religion is to help
mature the human spirit; yet many people are so
eager to believe in personal immortality, and in a
personal God who will guarantee the realization of
their wishes, that they have suborned religion to
give assurance that what they want will be
realized.

We have no guarantee that the seed we sow

will grow.   We do our best and rejoice if we
sometimes succeed.

The incident in front of the White House may
help us to remember that the spirit, although it
is a garden which requires much cultivation, flowers in deeds of mercy, understanding, and peace.

-0-

BIBLIOGRAPHY

Suggestions for the clarification of each chapter:

Part I, Chapter 1:

Burtt, Edwin, "Types of Religious Philosophy,"
    Harper, 1951
Burtt, Edwin, "Man Seeks the Divine," Harper, 1957

Chapter 2:

Blanshard, Brand, "Reason and Belief," Yale, 1974
Dewey, John, "The Quest for Certainty," Minton,
    Balch, 1929

Chapter 3:

Cloud, Preston, "Cosmos, Earth, and Man," Yale,
    1978
Nagel, Ernest, "The Structure of Science,"
    Harcourt, 1962 (This book is a more exhaus-
    tive treatment of the philosophy of causality
    and requirements.)

Chapter 4:

Overstreet, Harry, "The Mature Mind," W. W.
    Norton, 1949 (A popular exposition of the
    maturity concept.)
Maslow, Abraham, "Motivation and Personality,"
    Harper, 1954, 1970

Part II

Earlier efforts to recover the historical Jesus have been largely suppressed since 1930 by neo-othodox supernaturalism. Nevertheless, three progressive influences have been felt:

(a) Form criticism; how story forms indicate non-historical purposes. See: R. Bultmann, "Form Criticism," Harper, 1934.

(b) The stress on Kerygma, or message, rather than on myth. See: H. Bartsch, "Kerygma and Myth," S.P.C.K., 1953.

(c) The Dead Sea Scrolls, showing the misguidance of Messianism. See: G. Vermes, "The Dead Sea Scrolls," Penguin, 1975. (Also see Davies, below.)

Chapter 5:

Davies, A. Powell, "The Meaning of the Dead Sea Scrolls," Mentor, 1956

Davies, A. Powell, "The First Christian," St. Paul, Mentor, 1959

Chapter 6:

Goguel, Maurice, "The Birth of Christianity," Macmillan, 1954

Simon, Marcel, "Jewish Sects at the time of Jesus," Fortress, 1967

Chapter 7:

Nolan, Albert, "Jesus Before Christianity," Orbis, Maryknoll, 1978

Bundy, Walter, "Jesus and the First Three Gospels," Harvard, 1955

Chave, Ernest, "A Functional Approach to Religious Education." Chicago, 1947

Chapter 7 (continued):

Cadbury, Henry J., "The Eclipse of the Historical Jesus," Pendle Hill, 1963

Cadbury, Henry J., "Behind the Gospels," Pendle Hill, 1968

Part III, Chapter 8:

Cleghorn, Sarah, "The Seamless Robe," Macmillan, 1945

Chapter 9:

Gandhi, M. K., "Selected Writings," Harper, 1971

Mumford, Lewis, "The Conduct of Life," Harcourt Brace, 1951

Chapter 10:

Shi, David, "The Simple Life," Oxford, 1985

Chapter 11:

Bellah, R. N., and Hammon, P. E., "Varieties of Civil Religion," Harper, 1980

Streng, Frederick, "Understanding Religious Man," Dickenson, 1969

Miller, W. R., "The New Christianity," Delacorte, 1967. (Such writers as Schleiermacher, Strauss, Renan, Buber, Tillich, Bonhoeffer, Bultmann, Harvey Cox, and Bishop Robinson, while not entering the promised land of naturalism, reveal in this anthology why the old approach is no longer satisfactory.)

INDEX

Nolan, Albert 72, 107

T

U

W

YZ